For several years **Dena Attar** taught English and Drama in North Yorkshire. She has contributed to numerous books and journals, including *Spare Rib*, *Trouble and Strife*, *Camerawork* and *Sweeping Statements*, and is the compiler of a standard bibliography of domestic manuals (1987). She now teaches Gender and Education for The Open University, and lives in London.

In *Wasting Girls' Time* Dena Attar shows how, over the years, home economics has been renamed, reconstituted and manipulated to make it seem more relevant and valuable for all pupils, while in reality it precludes girls from studying subjects which might offer them more career opportunities, provides an entertaining interlude for the few boys who take it, and is in imminent danger of exclusion from the national curriculum despite valiant rescue attempts. With powerful logic she justifies this exclusion: home economics helps nobody, male or female, to cope effectively with domestic life; it is a tragic waste of time.

Also in the Virago Education Series
In association with the University of London Institute of Education

Read It To Me Now!: Learning at Home and at School
Hilary Minns

Un/Popular Fictions
Gemma Moss

Teaching Black Literature
Suzanne Scafe

Counting Girls Out
The Girls and Mathematics Unit, Institute of Education
Compiled by Valerie Walkerdine

Wasting Girls' Time

The History and Politics of Home Economics

Dena Attar

VIRAGO

Published by VIRAGO PRESS Limited 1990
20–23 Mandela Street, Camden Town, London NW1 0HQ

A CIP Catalogue record for this book is available from the British Library

Typeset in Great Britain by Burns & Smith Ltd, Derby

Printed by Cox & Wyman, Reading, Berkshire

Contents

List of Tables

Acknowledgements

The Open University School of Education Research Committee provided a grant to assist towards the research for this book, for which I am most grateful. I am also indebted to Jenny Shaw and Carol Dyhouse of the University of Sussex, who first encouraged me to continue the work, and to Jane Miller for her unfailing support and always valuable advice. The librarians of the Modern Records Office at the University of Warwick allowed me access to the archives of the ATDS and provided other help. Gemma Moss, Sophie Laws and Alasdair Richardson were there when I needed them, and make useful comments on early drafts. For practical everyday support I am especially pleased to thank them and Gideon, Joel and Raphael Attar, together with Kerry Harknett, Sharon French and Beryl Bolton.

I am unable to name all the students reading for the Open University MA in Education who provided a valuable and occasionally critical audience for some of the ideas in this book, but I would like to thank in particular Helen Glover and Gillian Hilton for their comments and insights. Edith Jayne and Wil Pennycook-Greaves also gave me material for thought. Lastly, I owe a special debt above all to the teachers and pupils who talked to me and allowed me to observe their work, who contributed so much to a book which I hope will in turn give something back to them.

Introduction

I came into this field sideways, one step at a time, but once I arrived it seemed the inevitable place to be. I have two versions of the journey, each holding about the same amount of truth, although one deals with ways and means and the other asks why.

In 1979 I left teaching temporarily to begin a research project which I envisaged as a feminist investigation into culinary history, asking who wrote the books of rules, for whom, and where their activities fitted in with a scheme of things which subordinated women but magnified the achievements of certain men. From there my work diverged into a commissioned study of the domestic manuals appearing in Britain between 1800 and 1914, which resulted in a book published in 1987.

During the years of bibliographic research I saw scores of advice manuals written mainly for women and girls on household management, the management of servants, childcare, domestic medicine and etiquette, along with schoolroom books for young ladies and many other varieties. The ones I liked the least, and most wanted to follow up, were a collection of school textbooks on domestic economy, domestic science, laundrywork and allied subjects.

This version could be continued as the story of one particular research path, which led on to a dissertation on the status of home economics in which I followed up its more recent history, and eventually to a schools-based research project. In that final stage I was able to set history and theory alongside my observations of real pupils in recent classrooms. According to this version I came to be looking at feminine, minority subjects in schools almost by accident. It lends a distance which I have used, and needed, on occasion. It will do, up to a point, but it doesn't really explain how, as a feminist and former English teacher, I came to spend so much time researching and writing about a subject I have neither studied nor taught.

As an outsider I have the option of keeping my distance. Most educational researchers have kept much further away, recognising that the least-respected subjects in the curriculum have little spare credit to bestow on any other professionals. The second version of my journey removes the illusion of distance, not because writing as an outsider needs an apology but because the teaching of domesticity has reached women's lives regardless of whether or not they experienced it directly.

I had always thought my own exposure to domestic teaching very slight: cross-stitch samplers, smocked aprons and a little knitting and embroidery in primary-school lessons while the boys were doing woodwork, followed by an afternoon of needlework a week for the first year of secondary school. Compared with many other girls, I was let off lightly. I was not expected to be competent at feminine crafts anyway, since 'academic' and 'practical' were divided into mutually exclusive categories, and nobody in those days questioned the division. In the second year parents chose for their daughters, or teachers chose for their pupils, between three options: Latin, German and needlework. It was understood by all that the decision should be made on the basis of girls' academic performances so far.

I learned a lesson it took me years to reassess: that clever girls could not cook or sew, while girls who could were not only non-intellectual but were the kind who dreamed of nothing more than being brides and home-makers. The content of those other lessons was puzzling, in particular the horrible hybrid of domestic science A level: what were they learning?

More recently, from nearly ten years' study of domestic advice and education, I learned how to open sash windows so that they let in air without creating a draught; I learned when it is expedient to keep the lid on a saucepan. For seven out of the last ten years raising children has taken a large part of my time, and whenever I returned to the textbooks which claimed to tell me how to do it, and how to manage my domestic life, I was struck most of all by their irrelevance. The motive for making home economics say what it was all about, for challenging its content and discovering its intentions, has come partly from this sense of a wide gap between prescription and reality, and of the gap created between women who were taught it and women who were not.

In the last analysis, though, there is something I cannot rationalise about the need to do this work. It has been a kind of exorcism, a response to the dull sense of suffering, of walled-in lives, which emanates from the old books used by girls in compulsory domestic classes and still seems present to me in classrooms and contemporary texts.

In the dictionary, 'to waste' is defined as to devastate, destroy, spoil, damage; to consume, use up, wear away, enfeeble, diminish or undermine. I have aimed to show, in this book, that the waste of girls' time is not a matter of accident or of small importance, however little-regarded the processes of diminishment have been.

1

A Cinderella Subject

This chapter is the work of a near spy, an act almost of treachery. The year the Education Reform Act became law I visited six secondary schools to talk to teachers and pupils about their current experience of home economics, and to observe and record a series of lessons. I was given a warmer welcome than any educational researcher seeking permission to disrupt lessons, however minimally, could have had a right to expect. The national curriculum was taking shape and all the signs were that home economics would be excluded. Some of the teachers I met reacted to my arrival as if I were a long-looked-for, often-despaired-of recruit to the rescue campaign.

'It's being left up to men to defend the subject,' one departmental head told me. 'Women won't do it.' In another school, when I introduced myself and explained the purpose of my visit, I met the response: 'At last the women's movement is starting to take notice of us'. Feminists were enemies of the cause, I heard, although they ought to have been allies. Home economics teachers were fighting a feminist campaign – as they saw it – either by defending a female subject, in the interests of their female pupils, from the contempt and ultimate neglect of the men behind the new legislation, or because they were working hard to change its image and content, ridding it of stereotyping and bias of all kinds. Feminists apparently did not know or did not care about these just claims to their support, because they would not speak up for home economics and, in the words of one teacher, were 'busy running it down'.

I had not come as a supporter. I found that observing lessons and talking to teachers at a time when they were in such a beleaguered situation put me in a difficult and painful dilemma. It was impossible not to agree

with the analysis that they were suffering the effect of a general devalu-
ing of women's skills, or to share their anxiety about the uncertain future
they faced. But my study was concerned with pupils' experiences, and
particularly with the ways in which fourteen-to-sixteen-year-old pupils
who had opted for GCSE Home Economics experienced a subject which
had a thoroughly gendered past but was now officially free of gender and
other bias.

Educational researchers have shown little interest in the current
teaching of home economics, although the history of domestic subjects,
especially in the period before 1914, has recently come under feminist
scrutiny. The few recent studies that exist tend to look at who studies
it and why, rather than at the subject itself. Its current claim to have
changed utterly into a useful, modern and bias-free subject has yet to be
seriously assessed.

This book examines home economics from a feminist perspective, but
a feminist perspective is not a single point of view. I argue that home
economics has a case to answer – not the obvious charge of sexist indoc-
trination, to which it pleaded guilty long ago, setting out to mend its
ways, but a more fundamental case of causing general educational harm.

My starting point is not the claim that the most traditionally feminine
subject in the curriculum must be supported because it involves and interests women and girls, or the argument that it should be condemned
for the same reason. I start with a question which has hardly been asked:
what is home economics? There are official definitions, textbook definitions, school and examination syllabuses, and there are conceptual
frameworks developed by teachers themselves for their own use. There
is a lay view which arises from the history of the subject, and which
teachers believe is obstructing progress. There is also the experience of
pupils.

What teachers set out to teach cannot be equated with what pupils
actually learn. The researcher in a classroom witnessing what happens
in lessons has the chance to peer into the gap between the two. The
following account does not and cannot provide evidence of what pupils
take away with them from lessons along with their tinfoil parcels, bags
and plastic boxes, although it offers some speculations. It looks into the
gap, and in so doing puts home economics into all its contexts at once
– which is how, like any subject, it is taught: in its historical, official,
theoretical, expert and non-expert, and above all immediate classroom
context.

The GCSE class described below was a mixed group of fourth-year pupils, studying Home Economics: Food. GCSE Home Economics now consists of four main 'aspects' or areas of study: Family (encompassing Child Development), Food, Home and Textiles. Food is the most popular of these, just as cookery (or the previous examination subjects 'domestic science' or 'home economics', largely cookery-based) used to be. The change from cookery as an O level or CSE subject to 'Food' as a GCSE Home Economics main study appears to have caught many pupils unawares. Nearly all those I spoke to in all six schools said they had been disappointed to find that they were spending much more time writing than cooking – one fourth-year class, midway through the spring term, told me that since the start of the school year only three of their lessons had involved practical cookery. Pupils' general disappointment in finding the course more theoretical and less practical than they had expected turned into a concentrated enthusiasm for the lessons which did give them a chance to cook. These lessons tended to be built up to through several sessions of written preparation. Pupils looked up recipes, wrote food lists and worked out time plans. All the work took place within the context of an 'investigation', as the examination syllabus required.

The class described here was carrying out a practical assignment as part of an investigation into healthy eating, a topic very much in evidence in all the schools I visited. Each pupil's task was to prepare a meal for one, and to explain in their subsequent evaluation how it fitted in with current dietary recommendations. They were not told what dishes to prepare, but most had chosen recipes from a narrow range of the cookery books available in the home economics room, using those books which featured wholefood or vegetarian recipes.

The lesson began in an anxious flurry with pupils and teacher tying on aprons, the teacher collecting in money (the pupils' compulsory contribution towards ingredients, standard in all the schools) and still sorting out ingredients on a separate tray for each pupil, a task which had usurped her morning break. 'Hurry, hurry, hurry – you've only got an hour', were her first words to the class. She also reminded them that this was an exam and they had to work in silence; she would be coming round to see their work and would be marking them for how they organised themselves, for their use of equipment and for the finished dish. They would be penalised if they failed to complete their washing up by the end of the allotted time. They needed to check their time plans, recipe sheets and ingredients, and could then begin.

The pupils began fetching utensils and food, working at top speed –

in the rush one pupil emptied a packet of frozen peas all over the floor soon after the start of the lesson. There was an atmosphere of tense, nervous excitement, probably not helped by my presence with clipboard and tape-recorder. I had met the teacher previously but not the pupils, and in the hurry to begin timing the practical test she forgot to tell them who I was. The following extracts are from my notes and audiotapes recording the intermittent progress of several pupils throughout the lesson, which began at 11.15 and was due to end at 12.20 – although it overran, as many practical lessons in home economics do.

11.30: Pupils begin work. Mark checks his time sheet constantly as he fetches his utensils.

Neil is making a salad using tinned chicken. He weighs out a precise amount of chicken from the tin, then cuts some green pepper into exact dice.

Lee still searching for utensils on his list. Lee peeling potatoes. Stops, checks list for next stage.

11.35: Dawn puts a pretty arrangement of lettuce leaves on a plate.

Sandra and Claire are sharing the use of a microwave oven. They take turns to bake their potatoes.

11.38: Dawn lays a slice of ham slowly and carefully in the exact centre of her plate, adjusting until it looks as if it is positioned symmetrically. She then slices a piece of cucumber, with a knife.

11.42: Dawn puts a neat ring of overlapping cucumber slices around the edge of her plate. She then begins grating some cheese, using a grater. She starts putting cheese on her plate, forming a decorative pattern on top of the ham. She continues to do this, slowly, for several minutes until she has used all the cheese. She has now obliterated her original pattern.

11.51: Dawn adds some salad cream to the grated cheese. She then places a single slice from a spring onion in the centre of her dish, and looks at it for a while.

11.57: Neil slices a tomato, using a food processor.

12.02: Dawn has now added some more spring onion and some tomato to her plate.

12.06: Dawn butters a slice of wholemeal bread.

Sandra is trying unsuccessfully to make some slices of apple remain upright in her baked potato.

Nicole checks the appearance of her pasta dish against the illustration in her recipe book. Says 'It doesn't look like that' and appears upset.

12.08: Lee has finished mashing his potatoes. He looks as if he doesn't know what to do next.

Twenty minutes before the end of the lesson the teacher told pupils that they would not have time to complete their own full evaluation of their work – the examination next year would allow fifteen minutes for this. 'If you know there were things you did wrong and could have improved on you should jot them down now.' They would have time to write up their evaluations in a subsequent lesson. Some pupils were still hurrying to finish their cooking while others were clearing away and washing up as the teacher began to check their work. Her comments usually referred to the appearance of each dish, but in most cases she challenged the low estimates of their grades which the pupils gave themselves.

TEACHER: [to Neil] What's wrong with it? You could have used a flat dish rather than a bowl, don't you see ... also your lettuce is a bit skimpy, but otherwise ...
[to Debbie, who is very disappointed with her pasta dish] It lacks colour, that's all ...
[to Mark, who cooked a rice dish] It's too squashed ...
[to Dawn] What would you give yourself, out of ten? Five? That's not very much, what's the matter with it? ... Why did you do the cheese like that ... why did you put the tomato that way up? You see there's a pattern the other side, you did the onions differently ... [Dawn's answers inaudible] ... But you did what you set out to do, didn't you? [Checks Dawn's worksheet] Ham salad ... where's the ham?
DAWN: [pointing to the cheese] It's under there. [Pause] It's a surprise salad.
LEE: [to Paul, after the teacher has seen Paul's work] Don't she taste it?
PAUL: No, she probably doesn't wanna.

When the lesson ended, informality set in, although most of the pupils remained in the home economics room, clearing up, looking at each other's work and talking. A male teacher came in from a classroom opposite and commented on the attractive smell of the room. He spoke to a number of pupils, and went round with a spoon tasting their dishes. A few pupils were eating the food they or their friends had prepared. Lee, who had made a lentil pie, collected a sheet of newspaper to scrape his food on to, parcelled it up and threw it away, untouched. Paul did the same with his stir-fry. The teacher's reaction was horrified and angry. She at once began protesting, telling them it was a 'wicked waste'.

LEE: But look at it, Miss, it's horrible.
PAUL: I've never eaten a courgette in my life.

In the ensuing argument the teacher tried to explain that they could have cooked anything they wanted, which they were prepared to eat, rather than waste food. Provided they explained how it fitted in with the healthy eating guidelines it would have been perfectly acceptable to cook, say, chicken and chips. Paul's response was that he had known all along he was not going to eat his vegetarian stir-fry, and had deliberately cooked only a small quantity in order not to waste too much.

As the class dispersed there seemed to be a prevailing mood of dissatisfaction. In conversation with me later the teacher said:

> I'd have the lot living here and put them all in the kitchen for a week and they would be really good ... The emphasis in GCSE is on the evaluation and they just can't do it ... as soon as you ask them [to give themselves a grade] they say, oh, nothing because they have no self-esteem ... What do we do to these kids to make them think they're worth so little?

The distress of both the teacher and a number of the pupils taking part in this lesson was real. The pupils' unfamiliarity with the new GCSE system of coursework and evaluation does not entirely account for it, although this was now only the second year the course had been in existence, and still the first year for this particular class. The problems this class was experiencing are deep-rooted and certainly predate GCSE. They relate to the whole question of what the content of home economics is, and what pupils are supposed to gain from studying it.

The teacher and the pupils both 'knew' the answers to these questions, but what they knew was not shared; there was a different knowledge on each side of the gap. The teacher, for example, thought that pupils understood they had free choice when it came to preparing the meal. It did not matter what the meal consisted of at all since the point was to analyse how it met, or failed to meet, the aim of providing a healthy meal for one. This made the actions of the boys who threw their food away quite incomprehensible to her, since they need not have cooked food they did not like (it was particularly poignant that she had previously described Paul to me as 'only interested in home economics because he likes eating'). The pupils, on the other hand, clearly believed they were supposed to select something to cook which had already been classified as a healthy meal. It cannot have been a coincidence that virtually every member of the class had chosen a recipe from the same two or three sources.

This led to two predictable consequences. First, pupils set themselves the task of preparing dishes which were unfamiliar in every way, so that they were dependent on time plans and recipe sheets for all their moves and could judge their results only by making comparisons – usually unfavourable – with the illustrations in their books. Secondly, they ended up with dishes which were of a type they believed this particular assignment required, but such a departure from their own usual choice of foods that some of them at least would not even consider eating their meals themselves.

Paul appeared genuinely hurt by the teacher's attack on him for wasting good food. She thought his actions were counter to the whole basis of home economics. He thought, not surprisingly, that she had just changed the rules. He had done exactly what he thought she wanted him to do – cook a healthy meal. The assignment specified nothing about eating it or liking it. He had not taken into account the teacher's hidden agenda – that while this was a GCSE assignment, her real purposes included persuading pupils to change their eating habits. As many classroom researchers have demonstrated, pupils know certain rules about lessons, acquired through long experience of schooling. They usually try hard to discover what is expected of them and to provide it. In this instance they suddenly found their behaviour criticised in quite another, real-life context – much as if pupils who had done well in a paper on English literature were to find themselves in trouble for not wanting to carry on reading their examination texts once the bell rang and they were free to go.

Dawn had made an exceptional decision, without reference to the vegetarian and wholefood cookery books everyone else had used. She was the only pupil who did not have to refer constantly to a recipe, and could be her own authority on the presentation of her meal. On the face of it her choice, making a ham salad and accompanying it with a slice of bread, was an excellent one and in the world outside the classroom would have made rather more sense as the solution to the problem of providing one person with a healthy meal than many of the more complex dishes other pupils were assembling.

But there was another hidden agenda, of which Dawn became more aware as the lesson progressed. It does not take an hour to arrange a slice of ham on a plate with some salad, even allowing for buttering a piece of bread, preparing salad vegetables and clearing up afterwards. Dawn managed to prolong her task to take just over thirty-five minutes. She did this with some difficulty, even though she took as much care as possible over the neat arrangement of her ingredients. It took her ten minutes to arrange some lettuce, a slice of ham and some cucumber at the start of the lesson, yet by the end she obviously agreed with the teacher's criticism of the messy appearance of her dish. Her painstaking work showed how much she thought neat appearance mattered, and she was not alone in this. In a sense she had shown more originality than any of the other pupils, and her inventiveness was confirmed by her suggestion of a new name during the teacher's assessment to take account of the now invisible ham.

Dawn's problem was that something quite undefined was expected of her. She knew this, and was trying to respond, but was in an impossible situation. In theory she had been free to choose a dish which could easily have taken ten minutes or less to prepare from start to finish. In reality her actions showed she felt she was expected somehow to use all the available time. From the teacher's comments to me afterwards it was clear that pupils attempting only a simple, quick meal such as the ham salad would not be graded as highly as pupils attempting more complicated recipes (examiners' reports for past exams confirm that candidates are given credit for demonstrating craft skills, although it remains to be seen whether GCSE examiners will continue to take this line; in some other schools I visited pupils were encouraged to learn the preparation of a dish which showed off several skills at once, such as a vegetable and cheese flan). If she had taken less time both Dawn and the teacher would almost certainly have been happier with her results, but that was not all that counted. Since so much time was allowed, something else, something unstated, was clearly expected. Dawn spent the time overlaying one neat pattern with another until finally little of her work was left to see. The teacher's comments, particularly the suggestion that she had done something wrong (put the tomato the wrong way up) served to confirm Dawn's apparent belief that she was indeed going to be marked with reference to the appearance of the dish in every last detail.

The criteria by which the teacher was evaluating their work appeared to be quite mysterious to most of the pupils. They took the fact that she did not taste their food to imply that she did not consider it edible (although they were expected to eat it). On the one hand she was making an effort to reassure the majority of pupils who felt that their dishes were failures. The teacher explained to one pupil who was especially upset about the appearance of her dish, a mixture of sweetcorn and rice, that she could have made substitutions for other ingredients in the original recipe which the pupil had not liked and had simply left out. She tried hard to convince another girl that it did not matter if her dish looked somewhat different from the photograph in the book. On the other hand, her comments confirmed what many of the pupils evidently felt, to judge from the immense care they took: there were specific requirements relating to the final presentation of a dish which they would be assessed by, even if they did not know what these were.

Problems of pupil–teacher misunderstandings and differing expectations are of course not unique to home economics, and have been explored in other contexts in recent research. Primary-school teachers observed by Edwards and Mercer (1987) appeared to believe in the principle of 'not defining explicitly (for the children) the criteria for successful learning which would eventually be applied to what they had done' (p. 34) – the reasoning behind this was that pupils' learning would be more likely to flourish in an environment where there were no apparent constraints. The specific context of home economics is different and unique in several respects: it has a history as a girls' practical subject and in seeking to escape this now unwanted legacy its traditional content has been partially abandoned, although the traditional framework remains. The problem pupils face in studying it, and having their learning assessed, is more than that of how they encounter and deal with educational discourse. Home economics has a persistent identity problem, and while pupils try to work out what teachers expect through deduction, guesswork and reference to their own experience, they also have to deal with the fact that it is apparently no longer the subject they once believed it was, without knowing precisely what it now is.

The crisis of identity within home economics has been intensified by the advent of the national curriculum, almost as soon as it was supposed to have been resolved by the introduction of the GCSE examination. I asked the teachers I met whilst visiting schools how they saw the present state of their subject, and how they saw the future. The discrepancy between their inside view of home economics and the non-expert outside view, the state of being thoroughly misunderstood, were common themes.

All the teachers I met were women. Most were anxious, angry and felt under threat, partly because of the proposed national curriculum but also because of spending cuts, the loss of disillusioned members of their departments, and what they felt was a general lack of support for their work. 'Home economics is in danger of being wiped away,' I was told by one teacher who feared that little would be left of her subject even before the new Act came into effect:

> The threat ... is not just coming from the core curriculum – what people don't realise is that there won't be anything left of the subject anyway. It's expensive, and there are staff shortages, cuts, loss of ancillaries, no time to develop new courses, discouragement to pupils, all to take into account.

Other teachers spoke of their determination to fight. 'Home economists are a fierce lot', in the words of one who thought that home economists as a breed were 'too fierce and powerful' to allow their subject to disappear from the curriculum. The teacher who expressed the least fear for the future told me, 'There'll be a riot if they try to withdraw home economics from the curriculum – especially because of *boys* taking it.'

Throughout 1988 the National Association of Teachers of Home Economics (NATHE) had campaigned for recognition of the value of home economics as a school subject. In a dramatic letter of appeal to Kenneth Baker the Association asked the Minister how home economics could be excluded from the national foundation curriculum when it was the *only* subject to embrace and teach 'health and safety at home, responsibility, self-reliance, survival, management of life perpetuating resources, protection against hazards to life, skills in analysis and problem solving, technological awareness and skills, preparation for life in general' (NATHE, 1988). 'We have too much to offer to risk extinction', the Association's President wrote at the end of the year, in an article offering encouragement to its membership and holding out the hope that, through the Design and Technology component, home economics might have gained a foothold in the national curriculum (Broome, 1989).

The belief that home economics would eventually come under the umbrella of technology was shared by some teachers I spoke to, while others felt they had the least affinity with CDT (Craft, Design and Technology) teachers and showed no enthusiasm for the prospect of joining forces with them. They saw other visions of the future: home economics integrated into science, chopped up and scattered between different departments, or concentrated in the area of personal and social education.

Several teachers analysed their plight with reference to sexism – their subject was not valued because it was to do with the home and with women's work. More often, teachers referred to a second cause: home economics in its present form was simply not understood. They complained that they were regularly confronted with a view of their subject which was outdated and stereotyped – 'Some people think we still just cook'. They were disturbed to find that pupils thought of it as a girls' subject, that other teachers were sometimes downright hostile, and that people in general failed to realise what it involved. In one mixed school a survey of third-year pupils' attitudes had shocked the staff who designed it, revealing that pupils – who had already followed the department's revamped syllabus for three years – still thought home economics was a girls' subject of no use for a future career, and that it was about cooking.

These arguments opened up two possible strategies for supporters. The one adopted publicly by NATHE, and by the majority of teachers I spoke to, was to deny that home economics was still a girls' subject and stress how much it had changed. They pointed out that there had been no 'boys into home economics' equivalent of projects such as GIST (Girls Into Science and Technology) – 'It's all "girls into science", it's so unfair.' A few teachers departed from this equal-opportunities approach, putting up a partisan defence of the interests of the girls in their charge, arguing that traditionally feminine skills should be given space in school and accorded equal value with the 'harder' masculine curriculum areas. Some felt that in a male-dominated school it was grossly unfair to the girls to make subjects like textiles more 'masculine' when girls had little enough of their own space. A third group combined these positions, wishing the subject to remain 'feminine' but also wanting it to be promoted to boys.

Pupils and teachers alike were acutely aware of the discrepancy between the reality of the syllabus and pupils' prior expectations. Originally the domestic economy syllabus in British schools was based on a trio of compulsory elements: food, clothing and shelter. These were taught almost exclusively to girls, as a matter of course, both theoretically and as the practical subjects cookery, laundrywork and housewifery, together with copious amounts of needlework. Although there have been various changes of name in the course of this century there has been remarkably little change to this fundamental framework. While pupils may specialise in one of the four main areas of study (Family, Food, Home and Textiles) the syllabus requires them to relate it to all the others.

Teachers were divided over whether they welcomed the change brought by GCSE, though some were extremely positive. One denied emphatically that she taught cookery and argued that she had not done so for years, despite training as a cookery teacher. She thought her training had been largely useless for the work she was now doing, which was much more valuable, using food 'as a tool to teach concepts'. She felt strongly that she would never want to go back to teaching cookery. Another teacher put it rather differently: the actual content of the subject was now irrelevant, since it was process which mattered. Knowledge now went out of date so fast that it would almost be a mistake even to teach nutrition, since it would be possible to teach it only in the light of current, inadequate understanding. It was far more important to teach pupils skills. These were not, as formerly, the craft skills of cooking but the less specific skills of investigation, analysis and evaluation which the new examinations aimed to assess.

Amongst other teachers who were less satisfied with the change, some were concerned that the diminished amount of actual cookery would be a deterrent to prospective pupils, believing that more would opt for the GCSE course if home economics continued to be taught in lower forms as it used to be, with pupils taking home cakes. The boys especially expected home economics to mean cooking, and felt the keenest disappointment. In practice most schools were starting to adapt their lower-form teaching to bring it more in line with the GCSE approach. Another anxiety many teachers expressed was that pupils had inadequate time for acquiring practical skills through experience of cookery and would find themselves unprepared for practical examination tests. One way to address this problem was by rehearsing pupils in a small number of recipes, even if this appeared contrary to the ethos of GCSE, so that they would have 'something up their sleeve' which they felt able to prepare with confidence. The teachers who did this said they knew they were falling back on an old-fashioned system: the alternative modern route taken by those more strongly in favour of the new syllabuses was to stress to pupils that practical work need not involve any cooking at all. The division between the old and new approaches was illustrated for me by two teachers who recounted their experience of a recent home economics in-service training day. They had listened to discussions about computers, technology, modular courses and evaluation. 'Then somebody mentioned food, and we were all shocked!'

When I asked pupils why they had chosen home economics they tended to give concrete reasons, implying that the content was particularly important to them. Boys, rather than girls, mentioned wanting to be chefs. Girls occasionally mentioned its relevance to future employment plans, such as becoming a nanny, but more usually offered replies like 'It's for when we get our houses and that'; 'Cookery ... it's the main thing in the home.'

There was thus a consensus amongst pupils and teachers that home economics was supposed to teach 'skills for living', but no explicit consensus, even amongst teachers alone, about the nature of those skills. Those teachers who had shifted the emphasis of their work well away from traditional craft skills talked in abstract terms about concepts, analysis and evaluation, in effect redefining 'skills for living' to mean 'skills for applying skills for living'. The study of food, as in 'Home Economics: Food', included some study of cookery, but this meant looking at how cookery skills could be applied in various contexts. It did not mean, as pupils persisted in thinking, that they were going to be taught how to cook, or even given many opportunities to practise skills they already had. But while practical tests were no longer supposed to be examinations in cookery, teachers believed that pupils who showed off their craft skills would be likely to score an advantage over those who did not. It was a reasonable belief, since this has always been the case in GCE and CSE examinations and the criteria for GCSE assessment in this respect do not establish a complete break with the past.

The resulting confusion engulfed pupils and teachers alike. Teachers who developed strategies which enabled them to continue an earlier system, giving everyone in the class the same recipe to use at once, coped most easily. They did this by devising some specific reason for cooking the recipes they handed out, such as comparing the nutritional benefits of two different recipes for fairy cakes, or treating the making of spaghetti bolognese as an energy-saving exercise.

When pupils were not told exactly what to cook they were either directed or expected to use the department's collection of cookery books, which set limits on their notional freedom of choice. The written authority of the book then substituted for the teacher's instructions, whatever the merits or idiocies of the chosen recipes. Some indeed were in a category of their own as recipes invented for cookery books, lacking any other reason for existing and reminiscent of the lexicon of obscure words used as answers to word puzzles, without a meaningful setting outside the texts which record them and for which they were devised.

The use of written recipes was presented to all pupils as normal and necessary, and with this as their starting point they were easily adrift if they could not follow their instructions – when, for example, some of the specified ingredients were not bought because the teacher ruled them too expensive. It was too late for pupils forced to make, say, saffron risotto without the saffron, to reconsider their choice or be told to improvise. They were called on to use their creativity and common sense at the final stage to put things right, not at the stage of choosing what to do when it was assumed they would need instructions from an authoritative source.

'Skills for skills for living' translates as a form of superior common sense, but the world of home economics is not a common-sense world. It has its own rules and restrictions, and any exercise of common sense which does not take note of these, as Dawn discovered, becomes a risky business once pupils' performance is assessed.

The rules sometimes spring from a need to construct home economics around a central core of factual information, which is not open to negotiation. But verifiable fact, convention, value judgements, even etiquette overlap in home economics to such an extent that there are many examples of arbitrary and inflexible statements about the correctness of pupils' responses. The stated correct answer to one specimen examination question on why breastfeeding should be preferred to bottle-feeding is that breast milk is easier for the baby to digest (SEG, 1987). Alternative answers, including 'it is cleaner', would be marked as incorrect, although it is difficult to see why this should be classed as a wrong answer in any other setting.

In another more extreme example, an examiners' report on a GCE Home Economics ordinary level examination, just before the introduction of GCSE, complained: 'A number of candidates served Victoria Sandwich cake as a pudding – it is a cake – and they had to be penalised' (JMB, 1986). There are no other circumstances where serving a cake as a pudding, a practice which is not dangerous, unaesthetic or even abnormal, could infringe a rule and exact a penalty from the cook.

Everyday life is meant to be the subject matter of home economics, but the real-life situations it constantly refers to are fantasy constructions, moral tales showing how people who have learned to employ a refined form of common sense ought to live. The faults for which home economics candidates are criticised are scarcely faults in any other context, but the achievements and responses presented as models of correctness for them are also curiously unreal. This is the inevitable result of imposing norms, absolutes and limits on to the messy business of real life.

This split between reality and unreality shows up in a mysterious question on a specimen GCSE 'Home Studies' paper which requires candidates to state two factors they would consider when buying a shirt for summer (MEG, 1988). Superficially this is a question which could be answered by anyone, but candidates know that there are right and wrong answers (in the marking guidelines one mark each is given for factors such as appropriate fabric/design, purpose, cost, washability). The question works on two levels, both personal and impersonal. It asks pupils 'What should a student of home economics take into account when buying a hypothetical summer shirt?' But it is also asking 'How sensible are you? Are you sensible enough?' Its intentions contradict its wording: the one thing it is not asking is 'What would you really do?'

In the artificial and bloodless world of home economics, rational beings make rational decisions at all times and decision-making, on however trivial a level, is transformed into an intellectual application of knowledge and skills which is meant somehow to be measurable. Poverty, religion and culture are routinely acknowledged and treated smoothly as variables along with other listed variables such as time available for housework and calorific needs. There is no passion, no politics. The denial and exclusion of politics in one recent textbook leads the authors to state blandly, after a description of the community charge (poll tax) as successor to the domestic rate, 'Such a tax is seen as a fairer method than the present system' (Barker, Kimmings and Phillips, 1989). What matters here is knowing what bills to pay: controversy is quietly suppressed.

Perhaps this is why home economics gets cookery teaching so wildly wrong. Examiners and teachers wring their hands over pupils' reluctance to try new foods – 'No dish would be acceptable to all, but an open-minded approach is advisable in the study of food', one group of examiners wrote drily in reply to complaints about the compulsory dish set for a GCE ordinary level practical test (AEB, 1986). Yet pupils fail to be inspired, either by the new approach of matching meals to consumers, taking all variables into account, or by the older system of rehearsing a fixed repertoire of dishes and methods.

In a study of efforts to improve standards of domestic cookery in Britain, Mennell (1985) describes the overall impression of recipe books used with school classes in Liverpool, Manchester and London as 'dull, stodgy and unimaginative', demanding little skill. This was not because costs had to be kept low, since the recipes required 'more utensils and better cooking facilities than the poorer working-class household typically had, and more varied ingredients than they could afford'.

Mennell's observations relate to the late nineteenth century, but they can be much more generally applied, and not only to school recipe books. His view that such books left 'no room for emotional involvement in cooking ... no enthusiasm, no sense of an aesthetic dimension' can as easily be used to describe the current situation in home economics classrooms.

Many pupils opting for home economics begin with an interest in food and cooking, and sometimes already possess a degree of skill. Most cooks, domestic or professional, acquire their skills and interests somewhere other than the home economics room – in a recent anthology of recipes and reflections from women about their involvement with cooking, not one out of over fifty contributors mentioned home economics as an influence or source of knowledge (O'Sullivan, 1987). When cookery is put into the rational domain of the classroom, where it exists as a means of meeting carefully ascertained and measured needs, with no room for emotional involvement and the aesthetic dimension coming well behind other considerations, little space is left for any expression of interest and enjoyment.

There is still a belief that pupils must inevitably enjoy home economics, especially cooking – an attitude which grates on some of the home economics teachers I met who found comments from other teachers along the lines of 'I bet the boys enjoy cooking' especially irritating. This belief does not square with the reality I saw of disappointed pupils leaving classrooms after practical lessons, looking heavy with failure. Their teachers do not think that enjoying cookery is the point: there are too many other points and concepts to get across in the time. The actions of the teacher who came in to enjoy the atmosphere and the cooking, at the close of the lesson described above, stand out for their very ordinariness, where nothing else was ordinary. No one else was talking about how the food tasted, or even behaving as if that mattered.

The limits of examination syllabuses and the artificiality of the classroom setting may also sometimes circumscribe learning in other areas of the curriculum, but this matters more in a subject which claims to equip pupils with skills for living. It matters a great deal for pupils if what they take away from home economics is a sense of failure, a lack of confidence, a belief that there are rules about daily life which they have not managed to learn and a method for organising their domestic lives which they are forever unable to apply.

The claim that pupils do successfully learn such a method in home economics has been accepted without question by many people, especially by women who have never studied it. A number of women, questioning my criticisms of it, have expressed to me a belief that studying home economics would have helped them to cope with their families and their daily lives. They felt that their own education had left them inadequately equipped, that they had missed something vital.

This belief is not based on any evidence but rather on a desire, a wish that a method or a system existed to lighten women's domestic burdens, something which schools should be able to teach. In the nineteenth century, even before compulsory domestic training for girls was intro-

duced into schools, a flood of literature was published which promised
harmony and efficiency in the home to women of all classes through the
medium of the domestic routine. Books on domestic economy gave
precise timetables for household work, while childcare manuals detailed
the timetable for looking after baby. Childcare was invariably kept out
of domestic economy, and housework was kept out of childcare – an
essential ploy, since if taken together they would explode the idea that
a sensible routine would make the recommended workload easy or even
possible.

As I have argued elsewhere (Attar, 1987), the authors of these manuals
and magazines recognised a need and responded to it, but this does not
mean they were really able to deliver what they promised. The need was
not answered by advice on how to be more organised in the form of
a daily timetable, nor can it be answered now through training in using
a checklist of variables.

We still want answers: people want home economics to be as useful
as it says it is. The feeling that something vital was missed out of their
education appears particularly to strike women when they undergo the
first shocks of childbirth and parenthood. There may be some basis for
this when topics such as nutrition, pregnancy, childbirth and child
development are separated out from science, health and sex education
and planted in the specific, optional subject of home economics, which
not all pupils take. It has never been clear, though, how adolescent
school pupils can be prepared for parenthood, nor what home
economics as a specific subject can contribute to such preparation.

For a long time home economics teachers have acknowledged that the
only ingredients of their subject which could not logically be covered
elsewhere in the curriculum are the now somewhat despised craft skills.
At examination level child study courses include such usual home
economics activities as meal planning and toy (usually soft toy) making.
Few people now uphold the usefulness of the former practice of giving
pupils dolls to bath and nappies to fold – as one teacher told me, they'll
be taught that in the hospital at the appropriate time.

In 1988 the director of the National Society for the Prevention of
Cruelty to Children, Dr Alan Gilmour, joined in with criticism of the
proposed core curriculum on the basis that bringing up children was the
core of life, and that preparation for it ought to feature in the school
curriculum. The Society put to Kenneth Baker the argument that more

child abuse would result if preparation for parenthood was not included in pupils' education. There is an obvious temptation to put forward education as a solution to child abuse (the role of home economics as rescue work is discussed more fully in Chapter 7), but this assumption that unprepared parents tend to become abusers, while prepared parents do not, avoids looking at other implications of child abuse: at power relations within the family, and the status of children in society. It avoids, too, the hard question of what kind of preparation would work.

The curriculum for most girls in British schools for more than a century has included an element of preparation for unpaid work within the home. Under various names it has justified its place in schools through its claim to teach really useful skills and knowledge, and provide girls especially with some necessary training for their adult roles as housewives and mothers. Coerced at last by feminism and ultimately by the law, it has changed its declared intentions and expanded its reach, and now avers that it prepares all pupils for all kinds of living. The claims that it does these things have never been seriously investigated, and have hardly even been questioned.

Home economics teachers themselves acknowledge that there is an absence of evidence to support their case for its inclusion in the curriculum. One teacher argued in a recent article that if home economists 'had spent time over the last decade researching and publishing evidence about the contribution Home Economics makes to the education of our children' they would have been in a stronger position to argue with politicians and fight for their place in the curriculum (Scarbrough, 1989). There is no such evidence. The claims made by the NATHE in their letter to Kenneth Baker are only assertions – it is debatable whether any subject can prepare pupils for 'life in general', and the claim that home economics does so rests on little, if any, proof.

I discovered in the course of my own research into home economics, in the process of assembling a picture of its past and its present, that the two most important pieces of the jigsaw were missing. One was any evidence of its contribution to the education or later lives of those generations of girls who studied, and are still studying it. The other was pupils' own first-hand accounts of their experiences. It is no great surprise that pupils' voices are almost entirely missing from the history of domestic education, since they were predominantly female and working-class. What evidence remains – though it is sometimes evocative – is anecdotal, fleeting, forever inconclusive. It combines acceptance and even gratitude with bitterness and anger.

While researching domestic manuals for a bibliography a few years ago, I was sent a letter by a woman who studied domestic economy before the First World War. Her class spent an afternoon a week on practical housewifery, which entailed a two-mile walk each way to and from the teachers' lodging house, where the lesson took place. There the girls were given the teachers' laundry to do, and were expected to clean the house. It was marvellous for her and her classmates, wrote my correspondent, to come across such things as carpets and flush toilets, which no one had at home.

My mother was taught to grate soap and to starch laundry. Women of her generation, at school in the 1920s and 1930s, underwent a fairly rigorous training in domestic work (unless they were among the mainly middle-class minority who went to select secondary schools – the various strands of domestic education in the past are considered in detail in later chapters). If they did well, they were awarded good housewifery certificates. We know little of what this meant or achieved for them, apart from the fact that it preserved gender differentiation and denied girls the educational opportunities offered to their male peers.

In 1921 Mary Ingham's mother, aged fourteen, 'had two full days of training per week, one in the kitchen and one in the laundry' (Ingham, 1981). She learned to use a scrubbing board and a dolly tub, with shredded soap, and came top of her class in laundrywork. Years later she was faced with a series of boring mechanical tasks instead of opportunities to use her 'proud skill'. Mary Ingham pictured her mother as standing desolate, with her obsolete knowledge, in her hollow world of home.

The great advantage for many girls of lessons in domestic subjects, especially practical lessons, seems to have been that they provided some form of escape from the hard work or harassment of school at other times. Barbara Tomlinson, at school in the late 1930s, told her interviewer that domestic science was regarded as 'a bit of play. It was a sort of afternoon when we weren't at school, as it were' (Summerfield, 1987).

The pupils I interviewed in 1988 made similar comments about courses which involved outings from school. They enjoyed visiting play groups or doing shopping surveys because they were away from the classroom, and that was sometimes enough on its own to make the course worthwhile. When I asked pupils who had enjoyed going round shops comparing prices about the purpose of the exercise, most said they thought it was a waste of time; a typical comment was: 'I didn't think there was any point to it really'. They would have preferred a different reason for an outing, such as going to see a cookery demonstration, but still valued the chance to have an afternoon out.

Another kind of afternoon out, a pleasant oasis of girls-only time in a mixed school, featured in the recollections of a woman at school in the early 1970s. She remembered 'the calm that used to fall over the classroom in Needlework and Domestic Science. I remember thinking that it was good to be away from the boys in these lessons' (Adams and Arnot, 1986).

Set against the romantic idea of home economics as a haven for girls, a view debated more fully in the next chapter, must be a consideration of its actual effects on girls' education. I have concentrated mainly, though not exclusively, on the last two years of compulsory schooling (when pupils take GCSEs, formerly CSE or GCE) because in those years the study of home economics is nearly always optional, and pupils who opt for it take a decision which affects their career and educational prospects.

Most of the pupils who opt for home economics are girls, although the proportion of boys has increased from one in ten in 1975 to one in nine in 1985 (the level and character of boys' participation in home economics is discussed in Chapter 6). At the current rate of change equal numbers of boys and girls will not be reached until well into the twenty-first century. Meanwhile it is mainly girls who, in their tens of thousands, are cutting out pictures of babies to paste alongside descriptions of the proper bathtime routine, weighing and counting baked beans or sweets from different branded packets to work out value for money, choosing what might be their ideal cooker or placing stalks of mustard and cress individually on to neat plates of salad – all activities I observed in classrooms.

The examples I have used in this book are taken from schools which are models of good practice, not bad practice: where teachers have a keen awareness of equal-opportunities issues and are, for the most part, taking a fairly radical approach to their teaching and their subject. When I visited schools I was not looking for examples of gender, race or cultural bias, stereotyping, sexism or other unacceptable practices in any obvious sense, although not unexpectedly I saw some all-girl classes within mixed schools where pupils had a supposedly free option choice, witnessed the usual instances of boys swaggering their way through lessons at the expense of girls or female teachers, and noticed texts in use which were certainly not free of biased material. I was less struck by these predictable events than impressed by teachers' widespread efforts to rid home economics of its worst aspects and re-create it in a form relevant to their pupils. There are undoubtedly schools where home economics teaching takes a much less progressive shape – craft teachers have been categorised in one study as more likely to hold traditional views about sex roles than other teachers (Kelly, 1987).

For any classroom researcher there will be moments when it is difficult or impossible to remain a neutral observer. The problem most commonly discussed is that of the effect of the researcher's presence on other people and on the activities under observation. My own worst moment came when I discovered something which shocked me so much I felt an upsurge of anger I could hardly control. I had been asking pupils what GCSE subjects they were taking, and one of them told me that in addition to compulsory maths, English, religious education, games and general science, she was studying three separate home economics subjects: textiles, food, and child development (examination boards usually allow only two subjects but using more than one board makes a combination of three possible). Apart from an afternoon a week of voluntary work spent helping old people, that was the sum total of her last two years of compulsory education. That such an educational outrage was possible in 1988 makes the introduction of the national curriculum appear almost as a much-desired deliverance.

If knowledge is power, then some forms of knowledge are more powerful than others. It is no accident that the least powerful forms of knowledge are taught to the least valued groups of pupils. Home economics is still taught mainly to pupils who are female, working-class and often deemed low achievers. While they are studying home economics, and sometimes taking more than one branch of it, they are not studying anything else – in spite of the rhetoric about transferable skills.

When domestic economy was first introduced into schools, one commentator wrote of the 'evil' of an arrangement which meant that

... girls whose only opportunities of intellectual training are those given them at these schools, and whose school career is necessarily timed to terminate while they are still children, should have a larger portion of their school hours appropriated to household arts which could better be learned with opportunities of household practice. (Webster, 1879)

The question which must be addressed by advocates for home economics is not just what good it does, but whether studying it can compensate pupils for the harm of missing other educational opportunities. The existence of home economics has ensured that boys' and girls' education has been differentiated in a host of ways; it has affected what is taught in other subjects, making the 'hard' masculine subjects more masculine still by preserving a 'soft' subject at one end of the curriculum. The creation of an expert field of study has affected all of us, not only pupils who study it. It has preserved within the curriculum the concept of domestic work as a separate sphere (home economics always has to come back to the home, wherever it ranges). The argument that it is a really valuable field of study, undervalued only because it is about women's work, rests on no convincing evidence and has never been generally accepted.

The report of the Education, Science and Arts Committee of the House of Commons in 1981 deplored pupils' almost total division, by sex, in craft subjects (House of Commons, 1981). The Committee noted that 'in the past, crafts have perhaps been something of a Cinderella subject'. Cinderella ended up going to the ball, met the prince and married him, and had a happy ending. Design and Technology, the new name for CDT which stood at the opposite, masculine end of the curriculum from home economics, now looks as if it is going somewhere. Home economics looks able to join it in the national curriculum only in the guise of its old technical components, cookery and needlework.

The Committee's reaction to what it heard about CDT and home economics was completely one-sided, showing an interest in the evidence presented by the Equal Opportunities Commission and other witnesses about the absence of girls from CDT, but no equivalent interest in the absence of boys from home economics. Its recommendations called for the Inspectorate to monitor girls' take-up of CDT, but said nothing about home economics. Such incidents are not just sexist oversights. They are indications of the worth home economics is perceived to have compared with other subjects, even other craft subjects.

This book may betray the hopes of anyone hoping for feminist support for home economics, but in the end that matters less than betraying another generation of pupils. Before the argument that home economics is undervalued and neglected because it is seen as a female subject can be accepted, the case for its value, apparently overlooked for so long by so many people, needs to be made. There is undoubtedly much sexist bias against it, but that does not in itself answer the question of whether home economics has ever succeeded in doing much more than systematically waste girls' time.

2

Girls' Subjects

The authors of home economics textbooks used not to mince their words. A book published in Glasgow in 1878 with the title *Domestic Economy for the Use of Schools*, described by its anonymous author as having 'grown out of some manuscript notes employed in instructing a class of girls in the elements of Domestic Economy in a Female School of Industry', contained the following catechism:

Q. What is domestic economy?
A. The wise management of a household.
Q. For what purpose did God create woman?
A. That she might be a help meet for man.
Q. Can a woman be a help meet for man without having a knowledge of domestic economy?
A. No; every woman ought to know how to make a home comfortable.

This extract is fairly representative of the sentiments which appeared in many of the domestic economy textbooks published in Britain in the last quarter of the nineteenth century, especially after 1878 when domestic economy was made compulsory for girls in elementary schools. Domestic economy was an essential study for girls, they reiterated. It was even divinely ordained that girls should study it, according to some authors: a woman's domestic duty was inseparable from her moral and religious duty.

'The Household is a divine institution ... father, mother and children form the Divinely appointed household', wrote Jane Stoker in her introduction to *Home comfort: a complete manual of domestic economy for schools and colleges*, published in 1876. 'A woman has her own special work to do in the world', wrote Mrs W.H. Wigley in *Simple lessons in domestic economy* (1878). 'Every woman is a queen, and her kingdom is the home.' The enthusiastic and apparently somewhat eccentric Mrs Wigley taught domestic economy in Wexford and was later appointed by the London School Board for a period up to 1895 as a part-time Lady Lecturer in Science for girls (Waring, 1985). Her textbooks on domestic economy employed gushing narratives – one book was called 'The Marshfield maidens and the fairy Ondina' – and her chief literary model was evidently the religious tract.

The message was more often delivered without such embellishments as hers, but the case for girls to be taught domestic economy was usually presented as beyond argument. Faunthorpe's *Household Science* (1881) was subtitled 'Readings in necessary knowledge for girls and young women'. The author was explicit about his aims:

> This is the science of domestic economy; and every English girl ought to know it well, for upon girls and women depend almost entirely the domestic happiness of men, and the economical management of their earnings.

The most succinct rationale appeared in *Longman's Domestic Economy Readers* (1910): domestic economy was 'a very important subject for girls to study, because all work connected with the home is woman's work'.

Teachers now need to keep their distance from such a dangerous past. In the late twentieth century the commonest view of the 'problem' of home economics is not that it is, but that it has been stereotyped as, a girls' subject. This view has the advantage of being able to offer simple and obvious solutions: more boys must be encouraged to study home economics, and all traces of gender stereotyping must be removed.

Stereotyping can be dealt with most easily, at a theoretical level, if its causes can be dismissed as obsolete. The strongest current defence of home economics implies that its identity as a girls' subject is a matter of perception, and mistaken or outdated perception at that. A *Modus* editorial in 1987 complained that 'If ever a subject was at least *perceived* to be "for girls" Home Economics is.' The occasion for this grievance was a press release Kenneth Baker issued to schools, urging them to persuade girls and their parents to consider non-traditional subjects in the interests of girls' future careers. There was a clear implication that girls were to be encouraged to pursue non-traditional scientific and technical studies at the expense of traditional 'feminine' ones, of which home economics was the supreme example. The editorial considered this both unthinking and unfair: 'Quite unintentionally the secretary of state is undermining the subject'.

Much as its defenders would like to discard its undeniable and uncomfortable history as a girls' subject, the current construction of home economics cannot be understood without reference to its past. This chapter argues that gender was never something casually added on, which can be as casually removed. Home economics was invented as a girls' subject, and this identity has framed its content and shaped its forms of instruction. The existence within the school curriculum of a separate subject for girls has had an incalculable impact on education as a whole: marking out one area of the curriculum 'for girls' has inevitably marked out the rest of the curriculum in degrees of suitability for girls or for boys.

There is nothing unfair or fanciful about describing home economics as overwhelmingly still a girls' subject, although there has been a gradual change since 1975, when the Sex Discrimination Act made it illegal for schools to limit access to any school subject to one sex only. In their first three years of secondary education, boys and girls in most coeducational state secondary schools are now studying it compulsorily; some boys' schools, although by no means all, have introduced home economics courses. From the fourth year onwards, equality vanishes and home economics represents the most extreme example of gender differentiation of all school subjects.

Pupils' option choices from the fourth year of secondary school onwards have been an obvious field of research for at least a decade because there is such striking evidence of gender differentiation (see, for example, Pratt, Bloomfield and Searle, 1984). The GATE (Girls And Technology Education Project) charts, widely reproduced (Whyld, 1983; Mahony, 1985), showed that in 1980 no fewer than 91 per cent of the candidates for public examinations in domestic subjects were girls, and for needlework the figure rose to 100 per cent. Since then the proportion of boys has risen, especially for food and cookery, and the rate of change is also increasing. The most recent figures, at the time of writing, show that 77 per cent of the school leavers in England in 1986–7 who attempted GCE ordinary level or CSE commercial or domestic studies were girls, although this almost certainly understates the proportion taking domestic subjects alone who were girls.

The 16 per cent of boys leaving school in 1986–7 who had attempted any commercial or domestic subject (Table 1) included all those taking accounting, business studies, home economics, childcare, needlework, shorthand, typewriting, and some computer-related studies. The explanation provided by the DES, when I enquired why statistics on commercial subjects and domestic subjects were collected together, was that this was done 'for convenience'. It is not considered 'convenient' to aggregate figures for other subjects in this way, of course; the one connection between commercial and domestic studies is that both categories cover subjects taken overwhelmingly by girls, and so considered collectively unworthy of much serious attention. In separate examination statistics commercial studies, especially now that they include courses in computing and word processing, generally show a less extreme gender imbalance than domestic studies. The proportion of girls amongst the candidates for domestic subjects at CSE, GCE or GCSE level is probably still closer to 90 than 80 per cent, although the gap is narrowing (Table 2). If the trend for more boys, and fewer girls, to take home economics continues as at present, equal numbers will be reached in about thirty years' time.

Within this pattern there are regional variations, variations between examinations and most of all between the branches of home economics. Table 3 indicates the differences in boys' and girls' participation in home economics in a sample of examinations set by different boards. There has always been more of an imbalance in O level than in CSE entries, probably because boys thought capable of taking O levels were more likely to have been dissuaded from opting for low-status domestic subjects. At

Table 1 Percentage of school leavers in England, 1986–7, attempting GCE O level or CSE commercial and domestic studies[1]

	O level	CSE
Girls	22	32
Boys	6	10

Source: English School Leavers 1986–87 (DES 1988).
1. Statistics on domestic studies were not collected separately.

Table 2 Percentage distribution of girls and boys achieving CSE Grade 5 or better in domestic subjects

	1975	1980	1985
Girls (%)	95.2	93.3	90.8
Boys (%)	4.8	6.7	9.2

Source: Survey of Examining Boards in England (Statistics of Education, DES, 1987).

Table 3 Girls and boys entered for Cookery, Food and Nutrition O level, by examination board[1]

	1985		1986		1987	
	No.	%	No.	%	No.	%
(i) *London*						
Girls	5,352	95.4	4,616	95.5	4,241	93.0
Boys	259	4.5	267	5.5	310	7.0
(ii) *JMB*						
Girls	23,682	90.0	24,579	88.0	26,489	85.0
Boys	2,762	10.0	3,379	12.0	4,556	15.0

Source: Adapted from University of London and Joint Matriculation Board GCE Examination Statistics, 1988.
1. University of London GCE O level 'Food and Nutrition'; Joint Matriculation Board O level 'Home Economics: Food'.

GCE advanced level domestic science is so overwhelmingly a girls' subject that there are simply too few boys for any changing trends to register as statistically significant.

The availability of home economics to more boys makes it possible to exaggerate the amount of change, but as an option it is now merely an overwhelmingly rather than exclusively female choice. In the school year 1986–7 there were more than a million entries for the O level examinations set by one of the larger examining bodies, the Joint Matriculation Board. Of that total, just one was from a boy taking Home Economics: Child Care and Development. Two more boys took Home Economics: Clothing. No boys whatsoever took another home economics paper set by the Board, in Textiles. The proportion of boys in optional Food Studies classes in the mixed schools I visited varied from nearly a third of the class to zero (with occasional exceptions – discussed further in Chapter 6 – Food is the one aspect of home economics relatively popular with boys). This pattern of rather less than evenly balanced classes in some areas, and extreme imbalance in others, gives a more accurate idea of the situation in schools nationally than the statistics which show one boy for every nine or ten girls.

Home economics continues to be, in fact, in many schools and colleges and at many levels, what it was originally designed to be – a girls' subject. This has not gradually emerged as a problem, together with the 'traditional' image of home economics as a girls' subject, in the course of a hundred years and more in the curriculum of state schools. On the contrary, home economics teachers only recently, and quite suddenly, appear to have seen the sex stereotyping of their subject as a serious and urgent problem. Their change of stance has arisen partly from a changed climate of opinion which, as a side effect of encouraging girls into non-traditional subject areas, is 'undermining' home economics. As teachers rally to defend their subject it is undeniably being transformed somewhat from its early function of teaching woman to be a helpmeet for man. Yet in re-evaluating home economics the concept of sex stereotyping has only limited usefulness, since it leaves some fundamental questions about the ideology of the subject unanswered.

The concept of home as a separate sphere has not only survived intact in home economics, but is its essential foundation. The separation of the world – and in turn the world of knowledge and skills – into the domestic realm, where women are relatively powerful, and the infinitely wider world beyond, where they are relatively powerless, is neither natural nor inevitable and is certainly not neutral. It derives from and reinforces the reality of a subordinate sex servicing society, the community, the family, men. Logically there is no way in which removing sex stereotyping from a subject based ultimately on a division of knowledge directly related to socially constructed gender roles can work; no radical transformation is possible for a subject which remains founded on a concept of separate spheres.

From within the (self-named) home economics community two alternative approaches have developed in answer to the problem of home economics' historic identity as a girls' subject. The first, now widely adopted, consists of an attempt to remove the worst aspects of stereotyping, particularly changing the focus of teaching so that it no longer explicitly revolves around the domestic duties of a wife and mother.

Advocates of this approach claim, with reason, to have achieved a considerable amount already. Barbara Wynn (1983) wrote optimistically of a non-sexist future for the subject and put the case that its current critics were being unfair. She argued that 'some feminists' opposition to home economics is often based on the assumption that an outmoded syllabus is still being taught'. This opposition, as well as that provoked by a 'disdain ... towards practical subjects', was in her view based on a lack of knowledge and understanding of what home economics involved, and how much it had changed.

Wynn readily criticised past examination papers and textbooks for sexist bias which she also acknowledged had not wholly died out. The basis of her criticism was that home economics had tended to glorify and ritualise 'women's work', as well as unquestioningly promoting particular values and stereotypes. Her answers to the question 'What changes are needed?' were down-to-earth, rather than given on the level of theory. She argued that 'home economics can form a progressive and essential element of the curriculum, developing a wide range of intellectual, creative and practical skills needed by everyone' and that its emphasis should be on 'basic living skills which everyone needs'.

One problem with this approach is that it preserves intact the idea of a separate sphere without providing an alternative justification for it. Another is that in appealing to common sense it sidesteps the question of how a reformed home economics can avoid promoting a limited set of values and stereotypes, even if it is an enlarged and somewhat different set from previously. Wynn's own practical suggestions included some which aimed to provide a more accurate reflection of contemporary reality, for example tackling 'the limited range of lifestyles assumed by many home economics texts', and others which raised issues connected with the subject, such as the importance of better childcare provision. A new ideology of home economics was thus implied, although not articulated.

There are inevitable contradictions in the anti-stereotyping approach which seeks simply to give people information and skills in order for them to make their own decisions about their lifestyles, and wants to re-establish home economics teaching around 'basic living skills which everyone needs'. The implication is that home economics, hitherto ideologically unsound, can now be reinvented as a pure subject lacking any ideological content whatsoever, but simply relating to people's (un-theorised) needs. This process of reinvention is one which, as I argue in the next chapter, cannot and does not work, because of the illogicality of its starting point. Trying to hold home economics together as a consis-tent subject area whilst abandoning its identity as a girls' subject can only mean reasserting a view that knowledge and skills relevant to the home are somehow different, separate, and to be taught apart, whatever the effect on the curriculum as a whole.

The concept of a home economics curriculum based on 'needs' has been challenged from within the home economics community by Hesmondhalgh and Timpson (1987). They argued that this 'covertly promotes a moral element', leading to a notion of a 'right' or 'wrong' content of home economics, 'which in turn encourages the idea of "ex-pert" practitioners and a deficit view of the learner'. They proposed in-stead that the concept of 'need', the 'shopping list effect', could be jettisoned in favour of an issues-based curriculum. In support of this argu-ment they provided a sample list of issues: health, pollution, energy, race, technological change, class and gender.

Hesmondhalgh's and Timpson's proposal offers a new vision of cohorts of specialist teachers formerly trained to teach needlework/tex-tiles or cookery/food, now making a point of teaching those aspects of their subject which bear on race, or class, or gender. Such a vision is a tribute to the heroic inventiveness and determination to fight for their subject's survival of some home economics practitioners but it still re-mains an unlikely prospect, not only because of the known tendency of a sizeable proportion of home economics teachers to hold traditional at-titudes (Kelly *et al.*, 1987) but because it remains tied down to the con-cept of 'home' as a separate sphere. It is not easy to see why one group of teachers in secondary schools should teach issues-based courses using 'areas of current and relevant concern' as a starting point, only to have to focus discussion and learning on conditions and events within the family or the home.

While an approach which seeks to eradicate sex stereotyping has effec-tively to ignore the ultimate reason for the separate existence of a subject revolving around home and family, the alternative defence of home economics against masculine academic scorn and feminist criticism is explicitly a defence of separate spheres. The argument here is that home economics represents a valuable, though maligned, female-defined sphere of learning which differs from other subject areas not only because of its content but because it necessitates a qualitatively different approach. Advancing this view, Patricia J. Thompson (1986) quoted the words of Dean Sarah Louise Arnold, an American pioneer of professional home economics, in 1903: 'we have come upon an altogether new classification of knowledge'. Thompson argued that the domain of home economics was 'Hestian', of a different nature from the male-dominated 'Hermean' sphere which constituted other, more highly valued fields of learning (the terms 'Hestian' and 'Hermean' refer respectively to the classical deities of the hearth and of the public realm). Although Thompson argued that home economics was never intended to be for women only, she also described it as a 'female-defined discipline', even as the 'other' women's movement.

The greatest problem with Thompson's apologia for home economics is her assertion that it is indeed a separate kind of knowledge, dealing with a separate world. In arguing that a different type of knowledge is embodied in home economics, that it is a subject of 'relation and connection' and that to understand it 'requires a shift from a male defined Hermean mind-set to a female defined Hestian mind-set', Thompson takes for granted the continuing existence of 'male defined' subjects which do not relate or connect, and implies that there are inevitable and essential differences between these spheres of learning and her own. Yet apart from the obvious differences of status and gender identity, which are clearly linked, it is unclear what if any cognitive or conceptual differences actually exist: Thompson offers no evidence to support this thesis.

The distinction Thompson makes between 'Hermean' and 'Hestian' as outside/public versus inside/domestic does not translate into real differences – apart from the teaching of craft skills which it continually struggles to transcend there is nothing in the subject area of home economics which could not, and does not, appear elsewhere in the curriculum, as its practitioners have frequently acknowledged. The unique feature of home economics is that it relates and connects its assortment of skills and facts in the specific contexts of family and home. While Thompson argues convincingly that the 'Hestian' sphere suffered unfair neglect because it was 'privatized, feminized and otherized', she takes for granted the creation and continuing existence of an 'other', feminine sphere, even equating this with the continuance of child-bearing. Thompson's defence of home economics requires an ultimate acceptance of the status quo, of a masculine 'Hermean' sphere which ought to move over but does not need to change, and of a divided world with no possibility of integration. Hers is no radical solution: it asks merely for a righting of the balance – 'Hestian' subjects to be given equality with 'Hermean'.

Thompson is not alone in misusing the rhetoric of feminism to imply that anything centred on women's activities ought to meet with feminist approval, nor in failing to analyse the nature of the 'female-defined knowledge' for which she claims the right to equal status and curricular space. In the last resort such claims amount to an argument that there are essential differences between the sexes, other than physical biological difference, which stem not from social injustice but from biology itself. The claim that 'a discipline defined by women will look different from one defined by men' is thus held to be self-explanatory. The difference is not related, as it might have been, to women's oppression, and without being analysed it is automatically held to be a good thing.

I do not exclude the possibility that an academic discipline could be defined by women, or that a field of knowledge could centre on women's activities and interests, but feminists working towards these aims have done what Thompson fails to do – start from a belief that women are an oppressed group, and treat the home and family as problematic. The romantic presentation of home economics as a woman-defined, alternative field of knowledge is not remotely reflected in its current state.

One clear example of a topic within home economics which could be a female-defined alternative field of knowledge is the entirely female activity of breastfeeding. The manner in which this is actually taught absolutely refutes any notion that women have been able to control this part of the curriculum for their own interests, or to make use of feminist method. While the aims of such teaching have been to preserve infant lives and health, and often to encourage breastfeeding, it is just as likely to have achieved the opposite result.

An account of a course in infant care in one elementary school in 1910 described how girls were taught 'the proper kind of feeding bottle to use', prepared bottles and learned about 'patent foods' (Campbell,

1910). Although the author, a woman doctor who was advising the Board of Education on the teaching of infant care, pointed out the advantage of breastfeeding to a baby's health, it is apparent that the syllabuses she described and recommended would have concentrated much more on the technicalities of bottle-feeding. If anything, it could be argued that the inclusion of infant feeding as part of the syllabus has played a part in the promotion of bottle-feeding and the gradual erosion of mothers' confidence in their ability to breastfeed which has continued throughout this century (Palmer, 1988).

The first obvious reason for the tendency of home economics to promote bottle-feeding, however unwittingly, has been that breastfeeding cannot be formally taught to school pupils, let alone practised by them, although they can be trained in the routines of bottle-feeding. Far from home economics adopting the feminist process of learning from shared experience, it is still usual for classes of adolescent girls, who are not mothers, to be taught about breastfeeding by teachers who are also not mothers. In this situation, teachers almost inevitably pass on a version of current medical orthodoxy which is hardly female-defined.

Textbooks and examinations reinforce this handing-on of male-defined knowledge as objective and not open to challenge. Breastfeeding is often presented as a morally correct choice, while at the same time this already dubious treatment of infant feeding is undermined by other confusing messages. One recent book aimed at GCSE classes asks pupils to explain why a mother *should* breastfeed, and also why she might *need* to bottle-feed (Nuffield Home Economics, 1985a). This attempt at correct medico-social evenhandedness comes more unstuck in the next chapter, which claims that 'the gradual reduction of breast or bottle foods should begin when the child is about three months old'. Such attempts to inform pupils about infant feeding, prevalent in other books I have seen used in child development lessons, are so inaccurate and misleading that they can only do damage, whatever their intentions.

In another example a GCSE specimen paper asks pupils to state why babies aged four to six months should have foods containing iron introduced into their diet, thus reinforcing the specious messages directed at mothers by commercial manufacturers and some medical sources to the effect that breast milk alone is not good enough for young babies (MEG, 1986). In the same paper pupils are required to state how a man can give support to his partner during pregnancy; while the aim here might be to combat the traditional image of distant fatherhood, the question negates the reality of lesbian and other mothers who do not have male partners. When there is evidence that even teaching which relates to the specifically female experiences of pregnancy, childbirth and breastfeeding is not now and has not been woman-defined, the argument that the entire field of home economics education can be claimed as woman-defined becomes difficult to sustain.

The version of home economics history which places its pioneers as feminist heroines is as partial as that which sees all women and girls as its passive victims. Feminist historians (for example Ehrenreich and English, 1979) have acknowledged and sought to understand the involvement of women in the construction of home economics without needing to celebrate it or claim it as an achievement on behalf of their entire sex. The following account takes issue with Thompson's unhistorical argument that home economics became a women's discipline, profession, and school subject 'by default'. The evidence leads to the opposite conclusion: that it was unequivocally designed to answer the question of what should be taught to women and girls. Its creation as a girls' subject, straitened to fit in with the requirements of female domestic roles and confined to a separate place in education, has led directly to the shallowness and rigidity, the narrowness and introversion, the obsession with 'correctness', triviality and miserable morality which have been its outstanding characteristic features.

In British schools, domestic subjects came to be taught formally to girls rather haphazardly. The 1870 Act for the first time promised an education to all children, which happened to include all girls. Once large numbers of girls began to attend elementary schools the problem of what to teach them – since virtually no one argued that they should follow the same curriculum as boys – provided an opportunity for the domestic economy reformers to step forward.

There is an apparent superfluity of terms in any discussion of the history of home economics or domestic economy, which is a reflection less of changes in content than of a continuing uncertainty about whether such teaching should be as practical as possible or ought to rank as intellectual training alongside, or even as a substitute for, the conventional academic school subjects. It also results from the low status of home economics which, as I discuss in Chapter 4, teachers often hoped could be improved on by a change of name. 'Domestic subjects', 'domestic science', 'domestic economy', 'housecraft' and 'home economics' all refer to the same subject, which has been renamed at intervals throughout the last hundred years although its material content has stayed fairly constant.

'Domestic subjects' included sewing, also known as needlework, now included in textiles; cookery, also known as food and sometimes included in food and nutrition; housewifery, also known as domestic economy or housecraft, now included in 'home' as in 'Home and food', 'Home and family'; laundrywork, sometimes taught separately, otherwise included in domestic economy, housecraft and now textiles; infant care, sometimes parentcraft and now child development; other peripheral areas which were once part of domestic economy such as hygiene, sanitation and ventilation, now part of 'home and family'; and 'thrift', the equivalent of consumer studies today.

There are two detailed histories of the early years of domestic economy teaching which provide a favourable account of its development. The most recent, by Helen Sillitoe, was published in 1933. The other, by Ailsa Yoxall (1913), was commissioned by the Association of Teachers of Domestic Subjects (the professional association which eventually became NATHE). These histories, like the section in Margaret Weddell's *Training in Home Management* (1955) which deals with 'the early teaching of homecraft', must be seen as partisan – Weddell was formerly chairman [*sic*] of the ATDS. Their authors were in agreement that behind the impetus for domestic subjects teaching in elementary schools was an anxiety about living standards in working-class homes – the official explanation (see, for example, HMI, 1978), although they also acknowledged that parents had good reason to suspect that some amongst the middle-class 'domestic reformers' were chiefly concerned with securing a better supply of skilled servants.

Recently feminist historians, including Davin (1979), David (1980), Dyhouse (1981), Purvis (1985), Lewis (1986) and Turnbull (1987), have provided more critical accounts of the rise of the domestic subjects, and their role in disseminating a middle-class domestic ideology through training in housework and exhortations about a woman's place in the home. There is nevertheless some common ground between the traditionalists Yoxall, Sillitoe and Weddell, and feminist historians on the official rationale for its inclusion in the curriculum. The generally accepted explanation attaches considerable importance to evidence that the original advocates of domestic economy teaching tended to blame conditions in working-class homes on the feckless and ignorant housewives who lived in and supposedly mismanaged them. The historians differ, of course, in their interpretation of this attitude.

Sillitoe (1933) described it as a simple misunderstanding:

> It was difficult for the ordinary well-to-do person to see that the housewife
> – especially the town housewife – was largely the victim of circumstances that
> were beyond her control. They were able therefore to fix responsibility on
> her with an easy conscience. Some of those early domestic reformers pro-
> nounced judgment upon the housewife for 'her thriftless and slatternly
> habits' [the phrase is Yoxall's] in speeches and letters of unmitigated condem-
> nation ... The presentation of a scapegoat in the person of the working man's
> wife and the picturesque exposure of her shortcomings on platforms and in
> the Press had, however, some compensation. It aroused the interest of the
> general public, and the interest and support of the public were necessary to
> secure reform.

In contrast, Davin (1979) argues that compulsory elementary education aimed 'to impose on working-class children the bourgeois view of family functions and responsibilities' because of a fundamental fear of an unruly working class, which could perhaps be kept in check if the family could be stabilised. Teaching domestic economy to girls was the most considered and deliberate method of inculcating bourgeois values of home and family, although the same ethos pervaded the atmosphere of the schools generally and was manifested in reading books for young children.

Of all the domestic subjects, needlework has always been the most difficult for girls to escape from entirely. It has the longest history as part of the school curriculum, and was taught in every type of establishment which purported to educate girls. It was the first school subject decreed by the government to be compulsory for girls only, when the Codes of Regulation now known as the system of payments by results came into force in 1862.

The chief features of needlework teaching were that it occupied a great deal of girls' time, at very little expense, and segregated pupils for a portion of the school day while the boys were taught more advanced mathematics, a foreign language or other subjects which were denied to the girls (for examples of timetables see Digby and Searby, 1981). Turnbull (1987), discussing the various justifications for teaching needlework which were put forward over the years, argued that it was used virtually as a sedative, to teach girls docility, keep them well behaved and quiet. Even in the nineteenth century the practical usefulness of the laborious stitching pupils were compelled to do was in question – the sewing machine had, after all, already been invented.

One eyewitness account of a needlework lesson at the turn of the century supports the case that training girls to be obedient was more important than teaching them skills or producing finished articles for use. Margaret Weddell remembered seeing a class of fifty infants aged five in a northern city school. Each girl had a strip of calico to hem, with ink dots marking the place where she should insert her needle. The lesson began with 'thimble drill', the girls having previously learned 'needle drill':

> At the end of the twenty minutes' lesson one stitch was achieved by everybody – no child failed to do one stitch, and no child made a second. No indication was given as to the purpose of the strip, nor indeed had it any beyond the immediate purpose of the moment. (Weddell, 1955)

Apart from the universal tradition of teaching needlework to girls, there had been little systematic formal teaching of domestic economy or of the other domestic subjects before the 1870 Education Act. Schoolroom books for middle-class girls from the early nineteenth century such as *The young woman's companion* (1814) included sections on cookery, home medicine and household management, but middle-class attitudes towards domestic work during the nineteenth century were contradictory. It was seen as woman's work, rather than ladies' work. Middle-class girls and women were under pressure from some quarters to learn the feminine duties of cooking and running a household, but from others to keep as much distance as possible from menial chores for the sake of preserving their class status.

Private cookery classes date back at least to the seventeenth century when Mary Tillinghast gave lessons to young ladies and published her *Rare and excellent receipts* (1678). Isabella Beeton was supposed to have taken a short course in pastry-making from an Epsom confectioner before her marriage, but such classes were by no means widespread or usual – her half-sister reportedly said that Isabella's action 'was considered *ultra modern* and not quite nice' (Spain, 1948).

The great majority of girls received the domestic training they were thought to need in their own homes or in their employers', if they were in domestic service. There were a few training schools which took girls, such as the National and Industrial Schools at Finchley which produced their own 'manuals of industry' in the 1840s, setting out in catechism form the duties of female servants. In 1842 the St John's Servants' School opened, with about a hundred female pupils and another thirty in its Brighton branch. The girls did all the chores except the laundry and were taught reading, writing, arithmetic, needlework and household work (Baylis, 1857). Places in such schools were not free, and although employers were enthusiastic and would have liked more such schemes there was no great supply of paid-for recruits (Attar, 1987).

The Committee of the Privy Council for the direction of education considered giving grants to schoolmistresses who taught domestic economy in the national schools in 1860, but decided against because of the expense and the difficulty of organising or supervising classes. They decided instead that schools ought to concentrate on needlework (Yoxall, 1913). Although a few schools continued to teach domestic economy, it was as a theoretical subject. More practical instruction was given to girls 'in orphanages and charitable institutions', who were usually explicitly destined for domestic service.

One of the earliest school textbooks on domestic economy was William Tegetmeier's *A manual of domestic economy*, published originally before 1858 and reaching its thirteenth edition by 1891. It was prepared 'under the direction of the Committee of the Home and Colonial School Society', presumably for use in their schools. Tegetmeier was a lecturer at the Society's training institution; he was also a naturalist and a friend of Charles Darwin. His *Manual* appeared to be written for the ultimate benefit of the labouring classes, but in the first instance for the benevolent middle classes. It included both a diagram of an 'ideal' cottage for an agricultural labourer's family, and an appendix of instructions for visitors to the poor which advised the lady visitor: 'You will point out to them, as occasion may require, their relative duties, and avail yourself of suitable opportunities of reproving open vice.'

At first the Boards of Education did not at all favour the introduction of domestic economy into the curriculum. This makes the arguments that the state set out deliberately to promote an ideology of home and motherhood aimed at keeping the working classes snugly free from rebellion and sending women back to their homes from the labour market – the critical view – or else aimed at improving their health and skills from a mixture of well-meaning concern and self-interest – the traditional view – somewhat problematic. Schools were obliged to continue teaching needlework to girls, but there was a good deal of resistance to the introduction of other domestic subjects, as Yoxall described. Teaching was offered first of all on a voluntary basis by the training schools which were set up and spread rapidly from 1873 onwards, but for several years practical domestic subjects, and domestic economy as a theoretical subject, were not officially recognised or funded.

According to Yoxall, the London School Board showed its prejudice against instruction in practical subjects by postponing fifteen times its consideration of the motion that '... it is desirable to promote a knowledge of plain cookery and of the household operations connected therewith as part of the elementary education of girls', before finally accepting it in June 1874 – four years after elementary education became compulsory for all under the 1870 Education Act. The domestic subjects were accepted piecemeal into the elementary-school curriculum, at intervals between 1875 and 1894, as subjects which qualified for grants under the Education Department's Codes. Pioneers such as Fanny Calder in Liverpool and Catherine Buckton, who stood for election to the Leeds School Board with the express intention of working for the acceptance of domestic economy teaching, campaigned for the subjects to be given serious consideration, to be organised and funded properly by the education authorities in their areas, and success was only gradual.

The introduction of the clutch of domestic subjects which eventually became home economics resulted less from deliberate centralised state planning than from the work of a coalition of interest groups. A movement to promote the teaching of domestic subjects came into being after 1870, meeting at congresses and conferences and helping to set up the first domestic economy teacher training college, the National Training School of Cookery, which opened in 1874. At the beginning there were a number of men involved in the movement, who appear to have come from three groups. Some were science teachers, such as Thomas Cartwright, author of *Domestic science* (1900), William Jerome Harrison, author of *The science of home life* (1882) and Henry Major, who lectured in chemistry and physiology, was an inspector for the Leicester School Board and also wrote several books on domestic economy. Others were doctors with an interest in promoting the teaching of hygiene, like the author of *Domestic economy for schools* (1881), Dr J. Milner Fothergill, and more notably Sir Arthur Newsholme, who also co-wrote one of the standard textbooks on domestic economy and later became President of the Society of Medical Officers of Health. A third group were clergymen, such as the Reverend John Faunthorpe, Principal of Whitelands teacher training college and author of *Household Science* (1881). There were also one or two eminent men who lent their names and titles to the cause; the most prominent was the Duke of Westminster, the first president of the National Training School of Cookery.

Middle-class women, almost by definition, constituted an interest group as employers of servants (although it is easy to exaggerate the extent to which the middle class was able to rely on servants: see McBride, 1976). There were other reasons for middle-class women to take an interest: teaching domestic skills and preaching the virtues of domesticity to the lower classes through the elementary schools offered a way of continuing by other means a tradition of middle-class female philanthropy, previously pursued through poor visiting, health visiting, membership of various sanitary and national health societies – even through the distribution of tracts. As Prochaska (1980) points out, middle-class women involved in philanthropic work – as many were – were used to training servants; it was a field in which they already had some expertise. (One teacher already referred to, Mrs Wigley, wrote advice books for mistresses explaining how they should treat and train their servants, as well as textbooks on domestic economy for elementary-school girls.) While women were still unable to vote, they were able for the first time to take a public role as members of School Boards, and it was natural for many of them to draw on their existing skills and interests.

Single women had a particular interest in the expansion of domestic subjects teaching at a time when the so-called 'surplus woman' question was much discussed and there was a pressing need to find new areas of female employment. The appallingly inadequate education of middle-class girls and the current heavy emphasis on domesticity left many of them trapped, at a time when some households were facing financial insecurity as a result of the economic recession and feminists were urging parents to face the fact that not all their daughters would marry (Bryant, 1979). The feminist campaign for access to higher education and to the professions for women was meeting fierce opposition; as Dyhouse (1981) has described, it was even argued that for girls to follow the same secondary-school curriculum as boys would injure their health. Against this background, some women looked for new types of employment which they already knew something about, which would enable them to support themselves without losing their class status entirely, and which would not bring down on them too much masculine wrath.

One solution was to write about what they knew. The journalist Eliza Warren, in *How I managed my house on two hundred pounds a year* (1864), inveighed against the 'silly sinful dogma' that it was wrong for a lady to earn her own bread and recommended to other women suffering widowhood or bankruptcy her own example of turning her housekeeping knowledge into paid work. She advocated both writing for the women's domestic magazine market and another way of capitalising on domestic expertise, becoming a 'lady-help'. The lady-help was to be a superior type of servant, who could live in and work as a cook, maid or housekeeper without abandoning her claim to gentility. Between 1870 and the early years of the twentieth century a minor vogue for 'lady-helps' led to the establishment of an 'Office of Lady Helps' in London (Prochaska, 1980) and even to a number of training homes for them – one in Cheltenham was called a 'Guild of Dames of the Household' (Marris, 1904), but such schemes reached few ladies and did not last.

Domestic education offered much more scope for the energetic domestic reformers. Ailsa Yoxall attributed the inspiration for the National Training School to a somewhat arbitrary event, J. Buckmaster's 1873 series of lectures on cookery, which started a craze for learning to cook. The novelty of these lectures lay first in their association of cookery with science – Buckmaster was no cook himself but a science lecturer and 'the science of cooking was a new subject for him'; a French chef 'with four women under him' performed the simultaneous demonstrations – and secondly in the idea of putting cookery on public display. They appear to have provided just the right excuse for those women whose activities had been circumscribed by the view that cookery classes, for a lady, were 'not quite nice' to begin taking domestic training seriously.

The National Training School, often known simply as the National, began as a cookery school in 1873, patronised by fashionable and wealthy women. From 1875 onwards it gave more emphasis to its teacher training courses, which were originally only three months long. The National's influence was enormous. It trained many of the women who went on to found or to head other schools of cookery and domestic economy around the country – such as Mrs M. Black, who became principal of the Glasgow Training School, and Marguerite Fedden, who was principal of St Martha's. It provided the first certificates for would-be domestic economy and cookery teachers and also exported its demonstration method, which became the standard format for teaching cookery in schools. Tegetmeier's *Scholar's handbook* (1876), commissioned by the London School Board once domestic economy had been officially recognised as a grant-earning 'specific subject', included an appendix of recipes used by the teachers of the National Training School.

The syllabus which girls in elementary schools were obliged to follow was divided into three stages. Food was studied in all of them, beginning with some vaguely scientific theory and ending with rules for cookery. In Stage I girls studied 'Food; its composition and nutritive value. Clothing and washing'; in Stage II 'Food; its functions. The Dwelling, warming, cleaning, and ventilation'; and in Stage III 'Food; its preparation and culinary treatment. Rules for health; the management of a sick room'.

Teaching was often by rote and girls were expected to memorise their lessons, which mingled moral exhortations with scientific or pretend-scientific explanation, and with prescriptive advice. In her chapters on washing in *Textbook of domestic economy* (1885), for example, Elizabeth Rice explained to pupils that 'Water is a *clear, colourless, transparent fluid, composed of oxygen and hydrogen gas* ... Soda is prepared by a chemical process from sea salt and certain acids.' Her 'useful hints' included sorting the washing 'in some room where the father is not likely to be annoyed by the sight of dirty clothes' and tying on 'a nice white apron' before folding clean clothes. Her instructions, and the questions for pupils to answer, were often minutely detailed: 'Give two directions to be attended to in hanging out clothes to dry'; 'What three things should be borne in mind when folding?'

As domestic subjects teaching expanded to take up more room in the curriculum for girls, practical cookery was provided as a separate subject in 1882, and laundrywork in 1890. The domestic reformers had a number of obstacles to overcome to achieve this, including opposition from parents who thought the teaching a waste of time. Because of the cost, the amount of actual cooking pupils could do was always restricted. Courses were criticised both for being inadequately scientific and for being too abstract and irrelevant to pupils' actual home lives. When the period of the Codes ended there was something of a backlash, with teachers in some cases trying to bring their subject down to earth by renaming it 'homecraft' or 'housecraft'.

Mary Hill in Sheffield set her pupils to polish their desks and clean the classroom windows. They practised the correct use of a broom and were even visited by a vacuum cleaner salesman. In her account of the lessons, she wrote: 'The work was always approached as some aspect of home life, never as so-called "Domestic Science" which, alas, is frequently very doubtful science with nothing "domestic" about it at all' (Hill, 1914).

There is no way we can determine how far the reformers seriously believed that tuition in domestic subjects would improve the lives and health of the working class or even influence behaviour, but such beliefs cannot have been supported by much actual evidence. Weddell, for example, maintained that laundrywork partly came to be introduced as a school subject because of the dirty state of the girls who turned up to cookery classes, and Yoxall described how a scheme of lessons in laundrywork was initially planned and organised by Mrs E. Lord, 'after taking private lessons from a laundress'. (Mrs Lord was made superintendent of laundrywork to the London School Board.) Yet as Smith (1979) notes, working-class children would often have possessed only one set of clothes. The schemes of work set out in laundrywork textbooks were fantastically unrealistic in the context of crowded homes without running water, and of the working lives of many women. The argument that working-class girls wore dirty clothes purely because they or their mothers were ignorant of laundrywork is no more tenable than the argument that women's ignorance was to blame for the low-quality diet of the poor, yet such ideas were used to justify the displacement of other school subjects, for girls, by still more domestic training.

One aim of the reformers in advocating domestic subjects teaching in elementary schools had been to 'rehabilitate' domestic service, as Augusta Webster put it in her discussion of the 1878 Domestic Economy Congress (Webster, 1879). The so-called servant problem, for employers, was not so much an actual shortage of servants as a shortage of trained and contented servants – employers complained that girls preferred other, less suitable types of employment. Newsholme and Scott (1894) recommended teachers to advise mothers that their daughters should be encouraged to become 'good domestic servants in preference to entering upon indifferent callings which frequently entail late hours, injury to health and exposure to temptation' (in fact servants often had to work long and late hours). Domestic service continued to provide a large proportion of the jobs available to women, accounting for 44 per cent of the female workforce in 1881 and 40 per cent in 1901, but it was in long-term decline and young girls leaving school were tending to avoid it (Burnett, 1974). Even as vocational training for domestic service, domestic subjects teaching cannot be shown to have been useful or effective.

Domestic subjects teaching was certainly intended in some quarters to have immediate practical effects, but it is doubtful whether it had much success in inculcating skills or altering patterns of domestic work. Working-class women had too little room to manoeuvre for their lives to be much altered by the instruction they were given in school. Its longer-term effects, meanwhile, were ideological in the sense that domestic economy itself came to be promoted as a subject worthy of academic study; that schools took on the role of judges of domestic performance, grading and classifying girls according to their housewifely skills, or lack of them; that an elaborate model of the daily round of work in the home was built up and presented as the way things should be done, down to the smallest details. Its most serious effect was that it controlled – and limited – working-class girls' access to a general education, to the point where it was accepted that half a girl's time in her last year at school should be allocated to lessons and practical work in the 'home-making centre' (Bidder and Baddeley, 1901).

Domestic subjects also served to differentiate the education of middle-class girls from that of boys. The conflicts which developed over the introduction of domestic subjects into secondary education for middle-class girls are discussed in later chapters: they were more explicitly concerned with the question of whether girls should have access to the same curriculum as boys and with the struggle, which was largely lost (Manthorpe, 1986), to construct a domestic 'science' which could substitute for other science teaching. It is no coincidence that the period when domestic subjects were taught without much controversy, from 1944 to the mid 1960s, was also the period when feminism was comparatively dormant. During that time there appears not to have been much debate about the acceptability of teaching housecraft – as it was then called – to girls in the secondary modern schools, and in a relatively calm atmosphere they cooked, cleaned, washed and sewed for a substantial period of their school days. Schools which had been set up with the needs of 'non-academic' pupils in mind were equipped in accordance with the recommendations of the Hadow Report of 1926 and the Newsom Report of 1963, with facilities for training girls in practical domestic work. It was all very matter-of-fact.

Enid McIntosh, chairman [*sic*] of the ATDS in 1955, wrote simply:

> Secondary modern schools are designed for pupils who learn readily through practical work, and housecraft should be an integral factor in their education ... Housecraft is also creative, and offers a means of self-expression and an outlet for the emotions. Most secondary modern schools make every effort to include it on the curriculum, and to give as much time to it as conditions allow ... (McIntosh, 1955, p. 77)

A four-year course in housecraft in a secondary modern school should give girls 'sufficient knowledge and experience of the basic techniques of cookery, laundrywork and cleaning to carry out normal household work'. In servantless households, chores had to be fitted in alongside each other (and along with caring for children, who were curiously absent from much domestic economy and housecraft teaching). The concepts of 'sequencing' and 'dovetailing' were developed within housecraft teaching, requiring that practical operations should be timed and slotted into a schedule. Practical examinations took up this idea – from the early 1950s pupils could take GCE Housecraft, but before the school-leaving age was raised in 1972 many pupils in secondary modern schools left before taking exams.

In the practical lessons I observed there was often considerable tension amongst teachers and pupils about finishing work on time. Many teachers commented that the time they were allocated was inadequate, but they would still have to plan work which left pupils in a panic about completing their cooking and clearing up before the bell went. Girls rushed about their chores anxiously clock-watching and with continual reminders from the teacher: 'You should have started by now'; 'Only half an hour left'; 'You've got ten minutes, ladies'; 'You should be clearing up by now'. These lesson patterns have not evolved by chance, or as an unavoidable response to rigid timetabling. They are based on a model of home economics teaching as itself a model of the housewife's day: girls rush to get meals on the table just as they are later supposed to do for hungry and impatient husbands returning from work.

Another new idea in housecraft teaching in the post-war period was aesthetics, as with increasing affluence 'taste' in furnishings and decoration became more of an issue. Housecraft teaching gradually came to have less to do with rescuing the thriftless poor from deplorable conditions, and more to do with creating ideal homes as a setting for 'happy family life'. Money was for spending, rather than saving. As Christine Daniels noted (1980), 'home economics became involved with the growth of the consumer movements of the 1950s and 1960s and the concept of the home and the family as consuming units began to appear in home economics examination syllabuses.'

Craft skills were still paramount – this was the period when home economics really did appear to mean 'stitching and stirring'. Home economics practitioners became even more concerned about teaching 'correct methods' of practical work, narrowing an already straitened subject further. Winifred Hargreaves's model of craft skills teaching is an example of the closed world home economics teachers inhabited at this time (Hargreaves, 1966). It included statements which make little sense taken by themselves (for example that for *all* crafts a knowledge of 'recipe' material or textures and flavours is needed) and an account of cookery which hardly squares with the fact that it is a worldwide, everyday activity.

Hargreaves maintained that accuracy, use of tools and machinery, cleanliness, working procedures and order, use of recipe and reference material, textures and flavours, pace of work, standards of finish and presentation, creative ability and experience as a buyer and consumer were 'basic to a knowledge of all crafts':

> Accuracy ... in a subject based on scientific principles pupils need to be taught that exact weighing, measuring, temperature control and timing are of first importance, then by their own experiments prove that sub-standard results may be due largely to their own inaccuracies.

Evidently she was referring to cookery as the important craft, yet elsewhere Hargreaves challenged its privileged status within home economics:

> The time given to cookery versus other competitors can easily get out of proportion. An exercise of self-revelation frequently shows that many pupils during a housecraft course spend 90 per cent of their time on cookery.

During this time girls' work was to be subjected to the teacher's appraisal, with no room for discussion of the criteria by which their results were deemed 'sub-standard'. Many teachers now are relieved that they are no longer 'likened to a judge at an agricultural show who looks for the best lemon meringue pie or victoria sandwich cake' (Coles, 1987), but some system of judging pupils' end products is still integral to the subject.

Hargreaves, in the mid 1960s, took for granted that home economics was largely a girls' subject, as did other authors well into the 1970s, when gender was at last discovered as a problem. The reinvention of home economics which this provoked is discussed in the next chapter; the last section of this chapter is concerned with the implications of separate spheres, and with what happens within schools where women teachers provide, and pupils study, a subject which is known to be for girls.

Whatever its supposed merits, home economics teaching displaces the teaching of other subjects which are perforce crowded out of the curriculum. As Augusta Webster noted in *A housewife's opinions* (1879), when domestic economy teaching was a new feature of the curriculum, while girls are studying domestic subjects they are not learning anything else. This was more evident to Webster at a time when girls were forced to take domestic subjects rather than, say, mathematics, science, geography or a foreign language, than it may be to observers now. Although during the examination years, from fourteen to sixteen, only a minority of pupils opt to study home economics, it is a sizeable minority: more than a hundred and seventy-five thousand girls leaving school in England during the school year 1986–7 had attempted CSE or GCE in domestic or commercial studies. Fewer had attempted physics, chemistry, CDT, French, history, geography, creative arts or even biological sciences.

Inevitably, opting for home economics means that girls have to drop other subjects. The problem of gender stereotyping can be restated as a question of access – as long as the curriculum includes such a clearly 'gendered' subject as home economics, how much access do girls have to the rest of the curriculum? It is self-evident that including any subject in the curriculum affects the time available to pupils to study others, but in this respect home economics can be seen as a special case, both because in the past there was a deliberate intention to teach it to girls instead of letting them take other lessons, and because offering a choice which includes a subject seen as 'for girls' presents pupils with choices which cannot be experienced as neutral.

School subjects have not acquired their gender labels in isolation, but in relation to each other. In the absence of a subject seen so definitively as a 'girls' subject' it would be easier for girls to see other subjects in the curriculum as less 'masculine', but the existence of home economics in schools changes the whole nature of girls' formal education, whether or not they opt to study it. It alters perceptions of the curriculum as a whole, and affects their access to education. There is some point here in asking the hypothetical question: what would have happened if domestic subjects had never been taught formally in elementary and secondary schools? The history of girls' education would obviously have been very different, and the social effects of allowing girls access to the same education given to boys unquantifiable. This alone has provided a powerful *negative* reason for teaching domestic subjects, and it was an argument put forward quite explicitly in the last century by those who saw no good reason to teach girls anything else (David, 1980).

In coeducational schools, home economics teaching has resulted in the creation of women-only and girls-only spaces. This in itself may attract girls to the subject, just as the men-only and boys-only spaces within which CDT and to a lesser extent the 'hard' sciences are taught appear to repel girls. In this context it is not so much the perceived 'femininity' or 'masculinity' of the subjects themselves producing an effect as the attraction of a secure space where girls may feel at ease as opposed to classrooms and workshops where they are likely to be disparaged, intimidated or even harassed (see, for example, Grant, 1983).

The sentiment which has been wrapped around the role of the home economics teacher in secondary schools is reminiscent of the image of women in primary teaching as substitute mothers, which has been analysed by Valerie Walkerdine and Carolyn Steedman. Both have written about women in primary schools trapped into impossible nurturant roles. Steedman (1985) writes of women 'imprisoned' by expectations of their mothering role: 'I didn't know about a set of pedagogic expectations that covertly and mildly – and *never* using this vocabulary – hoped that I might become a mother.'

Walkerdine (1986) argues that the 'quasi-maternal nurturance' required from, and offered by, women teachers disguises and denies power relations. This 'maternal nurturance' – fostered in and taught to girls and women – moreover 'pathologises activity and passion. Needs replace desire'.

These critiques of the quasi-maternal roles into which women teachers are trapped could equally apply to the advice which prospective or actual teachers of home economics received in the past. Teachers were encouraged to act in ways which could be (and often were) seen as usurping the mother's role; they were required to project an image which in some ways supplanted that of the mother.

In the mid sixties girls considering a career as domestic science teachers were told that they should be good at home crafts, and that a 'neat, pleasing appearance and an attractive voice are advantages since many children model themselves on their teacher and the impression of her personality may last all their lives' (Crease, 1965). Margaret Clark's book on teaching cookery (1970) spelt out the role of the home economics teacher in teaching 'socially acceptable' modes of speech, behaviour and dress: 'The housecraft teacher can do a great deal both by class work or by individual help to guide girls towards good taste in clothes.' Such social training, once taken for granted as well within the domain of home economics, may lead to a view of the pupil's home background as inadequate, or may be predicated on such a view.

Barbara Wynn (1983) argued that although 'good grooming' books for schools were still being produced, 'such biased trivia can be rooted out from the subject'. A more difficult question is how the image of the home economics teacher as well-groomed super-housewife, setting an example for the girls, can be rooted out. If home economics teachers are to teach 'basic living skills', as Wynn advocated, their image is likely to remain that of efficient would-be role models. They will continue to represent an approved version of femininity, whether their 'basic skills' teaching duplicates or contradicts what pupils have already learned at home. Teachers obliged to focus their teaching on the home and family will always be placed in a situation of challenging, or replicating, the informal teaching pupils receive in their own homes, usually from mothers.

Just as the home economics teacher appears to have been asked to fill a maternal role in secondary schools similar to the one which Walkerdine and Steedman suggest primary teachers were expected to play, so the home economics department can be seen through the writing of some commentators as a substitute home within the school, to be made available in particular for 'inadequate' pupils but also attracting girl pupils generally. Its function is almost that of the Wendy house in an infants' classroom – a retreat, as well as a place to play house.

These perceptions of home economics teachers and of the spaces where they teach as representing something different from mainstream teaching and classrooms seem to offer something valuable to pupils: lessons which are not like lessons, teachers who are more like mothers, classrooms which are kitchens or other areas where girls can make themselves at home. I have seen girls who were silent, withdrawn and clearly unhappy in other lessons appearing relaxed and confident as they worked with just a few other girls in the comparatively secure environment of a home economics room. Yet there can be no justification for schools where girls need to use the option of a girls' subject to gain some respite from neglect, hostility or abuse in other lessons, even at the cost of limiting their future career or academic options. Schools have passed to home economics teachers and departments functions which ought to be the responsibility of the school, and the curriculum, as a whole. The existence of a subject area which girls can claim as their own, where they can feel comfortable and which is easy for them to opt for, has distracted attention for too long from the overdue task of ensuring that they do not find themselves in such need of a retreat, and can see the whole curriculum as legitimately theirs.

3

Reinventing Home Economics

As home economics carries on through its forced changes, it sometimes takes on strange shapes. One fourth-year pupil I met, Maxine, who was taking GCSE Child Development, told me she liked her course apart from having had to make a stuffed cat. She said that part had been boring and she hadn't enjoyed it at all. In a different school Maxine might have had more luck: pupils in one school I visited were sometimes timetabled to use the woodwork room for the practical assignment which required them to make an item for a child. But Maxine's experience seemed fairly typical, since in many schools this feature of the syllabus provided the easiest way of constructing a link with 'Textiles', which was also a required part of the course. Making a soft toy has thus become a common feature of GCSE Child Development courses.

It can be argued that Maxine learned something about child development from making the stuffed cat, and course providers have to claim exactly that. It can also be argued that she would have learned more from a direct approach which did not use up so much time (a double lesson a week for half a term) and did not leave her feeling so bored. But Maxine's teacher did not have the freedom to choose the best approach, for her subject had been deliberately limited. The point of the stuffed cat was not so much what it taught about child development as what it taught about home economics as a school subject. In one sense, Maxine was compelled to make the cat by the previous Secretary of State for Education and Science, who had directly intervened in the debate about the framework for GCSE Home Economics subjects. Soft toys recently became so important an element of the study of child development because they helped to keep it within a particular model of home economics.

The newest frameworks for home economics teaching are the end result of a process which began in the 1970s prompted by the 'second wave' of feminism. The Sex Discrimination Act, which became law in 1975, made it illegal for coeducational schools to limit access to courses to pupils of one sex only. This did not mean that girls-only courses in home economics, or boys-only craft and technology courses, immediately disappeared. As Miriam David (1980) pointed out, the law was not strongly enforced, although the discrimination it was supposed to prevent was extremely widespread. A 1975 survey by HM Inspectorate had reported:

> ... all schools provided some special subjects for boys and some for girls. Girls were invariably provided with female courses such as home economics and needlework and boys with craftwork ... 'Childcare, child development, mothercare and homemaking are usually regarded as the province of girls'. (David, 1980, pp. 227–8, quoting a DES report of 1975)

There were no overnight changes; many schools simply ignored the law. Several years later the Equal Opportunities Commission gave evidence to the Education, Science and Arts Committee that on average they received one complaint a week in term time about the denial of equal access to the curriculum for girls and boys (House of Commons, 1981), which of course also meant that pupils were still being forced to take subjects 'appropriate' to their sex. A more immediate effect of the law was the pressure felt by some organisations, particularly examination boards and educational publishers, to repackage home economics as a 'mixed' subject. Even if in practice it was being studied mostly by girls and taught almost exclusively by women – men constituted no more than 1 per cent of the home economics teaching staff in 1977 (Arnot, 1984, p.43) – gender somehow had to be made to disappear.

In 1975 the Schools Council set up a three-year research project, 'Home economics in the middle years'. The first of its aims was to 'reconsider the place of home economics in the curriculum of 8 to 13 year-old pupils of both sexes'. In an article on the work of the team, Vincent Hutchinson explained that it decided that the focus of home economics ought to be on home and family. This neatly solved the problem of gender, simply by not referring to the specific role of women in the family or the specific work of women in the home. The ideal took over from the real once again: to replace the old imagery of cosy domestic perfection with the housewife in her proper place, a non-sexist world which did not yet exist was conjured up for pupils' consumption.

A shift of focus was not enough on its own to solve the problem of redefining home economics in the new context of equal opportunities. The traditional components of the subject were there because they were all aspects of women's work. Once this link could no longer be acknowledged, there was no longer any obviously close connection between the crafts of cooking and sewing, or between the theoretical study of food and that of textiles. There was an urgent need for a model of home economics which could supply some other link.

The research project, having found that 'the content of home economics was presented in too fragmentary a form', decided on 'a framework of key concepts related to the focus' (Hutchinson, 1979, p.76). The team 'identified' five concepts: nutrition, protection, development, interdependence and management. These concepts, they decided, were interrelated. At the time of their research the idea of integrated studies had become part of the most up-to-date thinking behind curriculum reform in many secondary schools. In adopting a 'unified field' approach, home economists were using the current educational vocabulary at the same time as working out how to make sense of the separate subjects within home economics as parts of a whole subject which made no reference to women's work.

There had already been many other attempts to construct such a model in response to the perennial identity problem of home economics. In 1973 the ATDS journal *Housecraft* published a series of articles on the 'identity of home economics'. The authors, Middlemas and Fry, put forward as their suggested model a diagram of overlapping circles which represented affective appreciations, psycho-motor skills, physical resources and cognitive appreciation.

On its own this could be applied to almost any field of human activity – building a wall, playing the saxophone, fixing a car, writing a poem – but this was not the authors' intention. Middlemas and Fry used their model to elaborate on their definition of home economics as 'the processes by which various resources, and the interactions of these resources, are purposefully organised and managed within and about the central focus of a residential building, to promote the development, well-being and interests of the occupant family'. They illustrated the workings of their model in a description of:

a meal in its fullest conceptualisation. A meal, as it appears on the table, is the result of physico-chemical reactions between food materials induced by the cook exercising her [*sic*] psycho-motor skills with the aid of appropriate tools and energy sources. Engaging in these operations with some measure of success can afford pleasure to the cook and serves to express her care and affection for the consumers. The meal, when eaten serves a bio-functional purpose but at the same time, the consumer can derive pleasure from the perceptual qualities of the meal and of the setting in which it is served. Any overt expression of this appreciation confirms and adds to the satisfaction of the cook and the whole situation at the table and accommodates social interactions. (Middlemas and Fry, 1973, p. 436)

I have quoted from this article at length, not because of its ludicrous language or its use of technical jargon to make us think we understand less about our everyday lives than we really do, but because it shows how attempts to explain the identity of home economics have served merely as disguised justifications for the status quo. Middlemas and Fry, in seeking to claim that home economics can claim a particular identity, constructed a model of 'difference' which could in fact have been applied to almost anything else. It could not in itself explain anything about the specific nature of home economics. The one feature which could be claimed as different, and as specific to home economics, was the territory in which it was located: the residential building with its occupant family, around whose development, well-being and interests the subject revolved. This essential limiting factor had simply to be taken for granted, since the claims of the building or the occupant family to such separate attention did not rest on any justification.

The 'fullest conceptualisation' of Middlemas's and Fry's exemplary meal time is as interesting for what it leaves out as for what it includes. There are no power relations, apparently, to trouble the mutually pleasurable happy family occasions where free-floating carers and appreciative diners meet and interact. The food arrives as empty of meaning and context-free as it is no doubt additive-free, for the cook to prepare purely in accordance with her own wishes and skills. I have never eaten such a meal, not because I have lived in especially quarrelsome households but because the constraints the authors fail to acknowledge have always been much more in evidence than the harmonious interplay they prefer to consider. The warm exchange of feelings is left in; the essential exchange of labour, which is not in reality a matter of mutuality or free choice, is left out. The language of the article is covertly coercive: this is what I should aim for at meal times. Life is supposed to be like this.

Even more striking is the authors' inability to explain the 'home economist' as anything other than the housewife. They suggest, as a humorous aside, that their model might 'interestingly be applied' to other adult members of the family (who are not specified) or to children, but continue: 'However, our particular concern here is with that one member of the family who usually takes the major responsibility for running the home – the housewife.' Thus one of their circles, representing cognitive appreciation, is also used to symbolise the *competence* of the individual', understood to be the housewife who 'takes' her role as if freely, rather than has it imposed on her. The 'model' turns out to be less an explanation of the subject than an idealised representation of family life, with the housewife's domestic skills placed in the foreground.

In a later example, Eleanor Vaines made a more elaborate attempt to produce a model, using the concept of home economics – which, she explained, 'is still struggling to define its identity' – as a 'unified field' (Vaines, 1979, p.12). According to Vaines, a considerable amount of energy had already been devoted to defining this field; she referred to the work of home economists from the late nineteenth and early twentieth century, and also from the 1960s and 1970s. This chronological pattern of anxiety is, as I have already noted, a curious but unmistakable reflection of wider concerns about the role of women.

Vaines's part in the debate was an attempt to bring together the idea of a unified field, which she maintained was a social system bound together by common themes, with a potentially contradictory idea of home economists as specialists. Her proposed model had five subsystems. The focus of the first was on content, looking at families and individuals as an environment, or in their immediate environment. The focus of the second was on tools, of the third the home economist's human development, and of the fourth the human services which home economists deliver. The title of the final sub-system was 'The mission of home economics', and its focus was the integration of the other systems.

There were divided views, Vaines acknowledged, on whether home economics was a collection of specialisms or some kind of whole – a division which could have real and serious consequences for practitioners, especially teachers. The problem with Vaines's attempted resolution was that it did no more than stake a claim that home economics could be both at once. Her sentences 'There are common themes which bind the whole of the social system of home economics' and 'Each home economist within the social system is a specialist of some kind' were given prominence in the text and printed in capitals (Vaines, 1979, p. 13), yet having read and reread her text I still do not know what these common themes are. Vaines was apparently unable to pin them down.

These various attempts to develop and explain concepts of home economics, with their complex abstractions, can make little sense to most people outside the home economics community. It is not surprising that they have made hardly any impact on the perceptions of pupils, parents and others. They deal with a problem which is simply not a real problem for anyone else. I have no trouble with the identity of home economics: I have not had to struggle with its meanings, goals or links. It costs me no great mental effort to construct a link between a pile of washing and a meal waiting to be cooked, or even between a stuffed cat and a small child. Why have the home economists and theorists found it so tortuously difficult? It can only be because they are forced to refuse the obvious links and invent others for reasons of status, of professional or academic standing, and ultimately for political reasons over which they have had little control.

A consensus of sorts eventually emerged from the many efforts to redefine home economics and produce new models of the subject. The separate subjects within home economics first had to be changed from practical domestic skills to a skills-based study of concepts, which could then be linked by 'common themes'. This was the approach taken in the HMI publication *Home Economics from 5 to 16* (1985), which categorised three main areas of home economics: home and family, nutrition and food, and textiles. The subject's objectives, in turn, came under three headings: values and attitudes, knowledge and concepts, and skills. The work of the Committee and of the Schools Council paved the way for the GCSE National Criteria (1986), which used much the same language and laid down officially how home economics was to be taught for pupils between fourteen and sixteen, without gender or other bias.

The GCSE National Criteria for Home Economics is the most recent redefinition of the subject, and the current official version for use in British schools. Its similarity to the earliest models of the subject is remarkable, but so too is its simultaneous attempt to distance itself from its precursors. The separate 'domestic subjects' of the nineteenth century – cookery, laundrywork, housewifery and needlework, with the later addition of infant care – have been replaced by the four major 'aspects', as they are called: Family, Food, Home, Textiles. But until the mid seventies the fact that the domestic subjects were linked because they were aspects of women's domestic labour did not have to be concealed. There was no claim that dressmaking, say, was in some other way intrinsically similar to cleaning, cooking or washing. The National Criteria, in providing a substitute link, came up with a new definition of the subject: 'The essence of Home Economics is the inter-relationships which unify the study of these major aspects' (SEC, 1986a, p. 1). As a definition, it is self-referring to the point of being circular – a quest for meaning rather than a meaningful explanation.

The document which sets out the GCSE National Criteria begins with this quotation:

> The most appropriate definition of Home Economics for the purposes of these criteria has been taken to be 'a study of the inter-relationships between the provision of food, clothing, shelter and related services, and man's [sic] physical, economic, social and aesthetic needs in the context of the Home' (*Institute of Home Economists*). (SEC, 1986a, p.1)

There is an invisible woman in this sentence. In its emphasis on 'man's' needs and the provision of services, it slides over the question of who the service provider might be. Immediately following this definition is a qualification:

> The later application of this study may be in the establishment of a *household* or participation in the industries and services providing for *domestic* consumption, or both. [emphasis added]

No subject could rationally claim to take as its field of study how to provide for human physical, economic, social and aesthetic needs, in total. What makes home economics possible is precisely the limiting factor of its emphasis on *home*. The National Criteria define 'family' as any household group, and 'community' as the 'society with which the individual and the family must interact'. Seen from this perspective, home economics seems a potentially vast, abstract exercise, but a paragraph later a much more familiar profile reasserts itself:

The needs listed [in the first paragraph] have been distilled into four major aspects: Family, Food, Home, Textiles. The essence of Home Economics is the inter-relationships which unify the study of these major aspects.

The only reason for distilling the 'needs' listed into these particular aspects is a historical one: the 'aspects' precisely correspond to the subject areas which pupils and parents already know about, and home economics specialists have already trained to teach. On this basis it would be unthinkable to leave out textiles, yet logically there is no particular reason why it should be given preference over building maintenance, or even electronics or pottery or vehicle maintenance. The sentence explaining the 'essence' of home economics switches attention from the four aspects themselves to the reason why all four must be studied together. The National Criteria do not allow the 'aspects' to be studied entirely separately for the GCSE examination. Candidates must choose a 'main' study, but must study it in relation to the other three aspects. The 'essence' of home economics turns out to be a necessary invention which substitutes for the earlier idea that family, food, home and textiles were simply the important ingredients in a woman's life.

The 'inter-relationships' between the 'aspects' are explained in detail in a later section (p.3) headed 'The unifying common themes of Home Economics', listed as human development, health, safety, protection, efficiency, values, aesthetics, and interaction with environment. Candidates follow a syllabus which comprises both a main study of a major aspect, in which 'the common themes will be present', and a 'common element' which is explained in these words: 'The inter-relation between all four major aspects brought about by the presence, in each of them, of the common themes, will comprise the common element in any course.'

The GCSE Home Economics guide for teachers (SEC, 1986c), the GCSE course guides and syllabuses produced by the various examination boards, and recent articles by and for home economics teachers, all seek to elucidate this paragraph by example and illustration. The course guide which first accompanied the National Criteria suggested that a candidate taking 'Home and Family' or 'Textiles and Family' as their main study could make a project on washing machines qualify for the 'common element' part of the course by using as the common themes 'interaction with the environment', 'efficiency', 'values' and 'safety'. The suggestion, apparently serious, for incorporating the aspect 'food' is that 'the removal of food stains and the position of the washing machine relative to other equipment could provide relevant links'.

Whatever the purpose or merits of this hypothetical project on washing machines, it is hard to see any reason for incorporating the aspect 'food' other than satisfying the demands of the syllabus. This particular link, between food and textiles, seems to have caused problems for many syllabus compilers. One 'Home Economics: Food' syllabus (NEA, 1988) offered other ideas: in a project on meal planning, pupils could look at 'social and cultural aspects of textiles used when serving meals'. This presumably referred to tablecloths, table napkins or possibly even oven gloves, and also represented an attempt to take account of the fact that as well as prohibiting gender bias, the GCSE National Criteria precluded cultural bias. In another example, a project on 'contamination of food' suggested that pupils consider the 'choice and care of kitchen textiles'. There are few possible translations of this phrase. It can only mean that fifteen- and sixteen-year-old pupils are to be put to study teatowels and dishcloths, including their 'care' – or, in other words, how to wash them.

The difficulties of the new GCSE syllabuses were foreseen by some home economics practitioners who tried to avert a situation in which the subject, in their view, would become virtually unteachable. The original proposals of the working party preparing the National Criteria guidelines were that pupils should continue to specialise, as they had previously been allowed to do. Candidates would then have been allowed to study simply 'Food' or 'Textiles'. The working party which drew up the draft criteria was thwarted in this aim by the Secretary of State for Education at the time, Sir Keith Joseph, who turned down the draft criteria in an unprecedented move and wrote to the working party that 'GCSE courses should cover the four areas of the family, the home, food and textiles and the inter-relationships between them, not just one or more of these areas' (quoted in Christian-Carter, 1985).

The furore about the draft national criteria and their eventual replacement was recorded in two opposing articles published in 1985: 'A brave new world?' by Judith Christian-Carter, and 'The sum of the whole' by Jane Hoare. The case for home economics as a collection of separate specialisms was made by Christian-Carter, who claimed that it no longer mattered if pupils concentrated on one of the four specialisms because from now on the emphasis would be on process rather than content.

This led her to argue that the *raison d'être* of the draft criteria was revolutionary. Home economics could be seen as 'an excellent medium for the development of a large number of learning skills'. This amounted in fact to an argument that the actual content of home economics was hardly relevant any more.

The opposing case put by Jane Hoare was that the draft proposals were simply reactionary. While Christian-Carter insisted that 'it was no longer desirable or practical to cover all aspects', Hoare asked:

> Why has the working party so relentlessly held to the view that the four aspects should be examined separately? At a time when curriculum innovation and development is concerned with bridging subject barriers it seems sad that home economics should be striving to divide its own content into artificial segments based on tradition.

The efforts made by each side to present their own case as progressive, and their opponents' as reactionary, disguised the material basis of the struggle. The separate-subjects advocates were concerned for the career prospects of specialist staff such as needlework teachers who would find it difficult to teach the new combined-aspects course (although some retraining courses were offered to them). The combined-subjects advocates knew that if home economics teachers remained strict specialists, many would lose their jobs anyway. As Christian-Carter pointed out with some bitterness, the other side's position was more politically expedient than her own. Schools were not prepared to offer the same number of separate subjects under the home economics banner as they would offer under science or technology. Home economists could not rely on the necessary support for extra staff and resources.

The combined approach, which presented itself as new and progressive, had an entirely reactionary effect – as Sir Keith, notorious for his views on the 'cycle of deprivation' and the inadequacy of working-class home life and parenting, no doubt intended. The effect of the new approach was that pupils had to stay constantly aware of the 'domestic' basis of the subject. There were one or two exceptions amongst the new syllabuses, particularly those which seemed intended to cater partly for the vocational needs of boys, who have traditionally opted for cookery courses with a view to a career in catering when they have taken home economics. Most of the other new syllabuses steered pupils towards a study of food *within* the home and for the family, however that unit was defined. Textiles were treated similarly, and pupils studying child development or the family were obliged to focus considerable attention on clothing and diet.

Some examination boards provided grids in their syllabus booklets to help teachers understand how the aspects, themes, elements and essence of the new subject could be assembled. Pupils studying child development who made toys, clothes, posters, games and meals could score ticks under the 'themes' health, safety, efficiency, values, aesthetics and interaction with the environment, as well as under the other 'aspects' home, food and textiles (LEAG, 1988, p. 350). It became necessary for Maxine to make her stuffed cat.

With home economics now so afraid of its own content, so reluctant to state clearly what pupils must learn, a larger responsibility passes to pupils themselves. A gigantic, farcical game is being played out in school and outside, as pupils collude with their teachers in constructing the new version of home economics as serious and worthwhile. They are sent carrying clipboards and assignment 'briefs' into supermarkets and shopping centres, into restaurants and takeaways, to compare contents and prices. Afterwards they produce detached reports discussing 'value for money', and can – sometimes – explain the purpose of their investigation. They can also, much more readily, explain why such an exercise has little bearing on real life, why they learned nothing from it and are amused at the idea of finding out for the first time through their surveys that corner shops are more expensive than supermarkets. They do not expect their findings to change their future behaviour. 'My Mum shops at Sainsbury's so I would. I think you just go to wherever you go.'

When the theme is 'safety', and they are told not to let an electrical flex trail over a gas cooker, they say charitably that the lesson 'could be useful for someone else'. In self-defence, they redirect the material of the course when it is so insultingly low-level – one GCSE textbook even tells pupils: 'Do not mix cloths used for washing-up, cleaning the floor, cleaning the toilet and bathroom' (Barker, Kimmings and Phillips, 1989, p. 133).

My overwhelming impression of the new home economics is of bad faith. The open-ended investigations which feature in most courses turn out not to be open at all; they are part of the elaborate construction which has been built around the old content, which is still there, still – as it has to be – culturally constrained, and still not open to negotiation.

The following example is an attempt by one head of a home

economics department, who was also an examiner, to devise work for Child Development courses which can fulfil the 'common element' requirement at the same time as meeting the needs of the GCSE criteria in general. All GCSE examinations and syllabuses are now obliged to 'differentiate' to allow for an assessment of the achievements of pupils of different ability levels. June Scarbrough's proposed assignment brief aimed to do this, and it also referred directly to the 'aims' of home economics listed in the National Criteria.

This sample assignment began with a question for pupils to answer: 'What methods do parents use to physically carry their young?' (Scarbrough, 1987). The author was able to explain easily enough how 'Textiles' could form part of the 'common element': 'materials/fabrics used e.g. slings, shawls, etc.'. The link with 'family' was suggested vaguely as – 'family patterns, organization, effects of culture, etc.' The link with food appeared quite extraordinarily as 'needs of nursing mothers, e.g. prams versus baby carriers, etc.' As the focus was on the needs of the mother rather than those of the infant, for 'food' to be included at all the author was forced to classify nursing mothers themselves as food.

What pupils were supposed to establish about the needs of nursing mothers, as opposed to non-nursing mothers or anyone else, when using prams or baby-carriers can be understood only in relation to the author's assumptions. She was presumably making a connection between breastfeeding and carrying a baby around permanently attached in a carrier, even though in contemporary Britain such a connection is largely a matter of fashion and ideology. Particular groups of middle-class mothers have been portrayed in recent years as both more inclined to breastfeed and more inclined to use baby slings. This is by no means a necessary connection. Babies in slings and carriers also appear in somewhat idealised images of motherhood in less-developed countries, as illustrated in one Nuffield Home Economics course book (1985a, p.11); the mothers portrayed in such 'natural' roles would be assumed to breastfeed their infants. These connections are completely extraneous to the question, yet without them it is hard to see how pupils could find anything sensible to say for this section of their assignment.

The next stage of the assignment required pupils to survey a sample of from two to four parents to discover how they carried their infants, and then to ask questions about the cost, method of purchase, method of cleaning and storage of the carrier. For 'very able pupils' an extra assignment offered a chance to excel: 'Evaluate the emotional satisfaction infants experience when they are in *constant body contact* with their *parent*' [emphasis added].

Substituting the gender-free 'parent' for 'mother' here satisfies the requirements of the National Criteria, but at the cost of making the question nonsensical. It cannot sensibly refer to an infant's 'constant body contact' with a 'parent', regardless of gender, rather than with its mother. But this incongruous literal compliance with the criteria is not the only problem with this assignment for the hapless pupil visiting the baby clinic or following a baby and its parent around collecting data. Evaluating the 'emotional satisfaction infants experience' is no easy task for mature adults, parents or paediatricians. The discovery Scarbrough presumably intended pupils to make is that, as some books claim, infants carried around all the time by their 'parents' cry less than babies in prams (an assertion to be found in some home economics textbooks: see Nuffield Home Economics, 1985a, p. 11).

Only those pupils lucky enough to chance on a sample of babies who conformed to this expected pattern of behaviour, and able to understand what the author had in mind, could have made sense of this assignment. Others would have faced an utterly bewildering task: their best strategy would probably have been to copy out extracts from the literature which claims that elsewhere in the world there are babies who are kept constantly with their mothers, and are never known to cry.

Other parts of the assignment told pupils to relate the results of their survey to the family, home, food and textiles, and to 'explain the links between family, home, food and textiles'. In this way the assignment could fulfil the first of the 'Aims' of home economics given in the National Criteria: 'To develop pupils' awareness of the inter-relationships within Home Economics' (SEC, 1986a, p.2). Explaining the requirements of the syllabus in itself becomes one of the tasks pupils face when they study GCSE Home Economics. As pupils are unlikely to discover for themselves that 'textiles' and 'food' have some inevitable interrelationship in the context of a study of ways of carrying infants, the best way of equipping them to cope with this aim would probably be to give them the list of 'common themes' to memorise. Rote-learning would offer them the surest path through this maze of spuriously progressive education.

The fundamental dishonesty which now underlies home economics goes well beyond the contrast between its elaborate structures and its actual content, which results in the study of providing for 'human physical, economic, social and aesthetic needs' coming down to earth as a study of dishcloths – like changing ends of a telescope. It goes beyond the careful exclusion of gender from contexts where it would appear to have a legitimate place. The integrity of home economics teaching is undermined most of all by the emphasis on 'open-ended' questions and assignments, which in fact conceal implicit assumptions. The switch from content to process, from telling pupils how to live to inviting them to explore ways of living, is based on a message purportedly free of bias which is ultimately a false one: that any given answer could be right. Pupils know, of course, that there are still right answers, and that home economics teachers and examiners know these right answers in advance.

Sometimes an awareness of this double-think threatens to break through the neutered, flattened surfaces of home economics texts. The chapter on 'design' in a Nuffield Home Economics course book includes a photograph of a three-piece suite (1985a, p. 123). The accompanying teacher's book explains the point of this photograph and another one alongside it:

> These photographs show examples of what is generally recognised to be good and bad design. You could discuss these pictures with your pupils. What is it that makes the Dartington jars in figure 15.1 so pleasing? Why is the Italian three-piece suite in figure 15.5 so awful? Do any pupils like it? Such responses are mainly subjective, and it should not be considered 'wrong' to like it. (1985b, p. 169)

It is this extract's blatant dishonesty that makes it so awful, although it is only a more-than-usually-explicit version of the open-and-shut ideology of home economics in general. The authors make a revealing distinction between the pupils' 'mainly subjective' responses and their own, in collusion with the teacher, which are presumed to be objective. While they make it clear that it would really be wrong to like the awful suite, they also explain that it would be better not to let the pupils know this directly. The concepts 'generally recognised', 'good', 'bad', 'awful', and 'pleasing' are used casually, without a context, as if they explain themselves and are not bound to historical periods and such awkward categories as class and cultural grouping. The passage incites teachers to a deliberate deception, which if it worked would end up as a tortuous way of telling pupils what teachers think is good design. Such attempts at concealment in the cause of open, 'discovery' learning depend on pupils' skills in working out what teacher really has in mind.

It is usually not difficult for pupils to work out the right answers, even when they are asked, with a show of democratic inclusiveness, to state what they really think. Another textbook from a popular series reprinted in 1985 – a book Wynn (1983) singled out for praise for its non-sexist approach – had this to say about childcare:

> Until quite recently it was accepted as normal that nearly all mothers who had children should stay at home to look after them. As long as the mother wants to do this and is able to provide a warm, affectionate and interesting family life, this is probably the best background a child can have, particularly in the first few years of his life. (McGrath, 1980, p. 159)

Pupils were then asked whether, if they had two children under five and enough money, they would want to go out to work, and in what circumstances they thought mothers 'really' needed help in caring for their children. The pretence of inviting discussion traps girls (at least there is no pretence that the questions address boys too) into declaring themselves in favour of full-time motherhood, unless they are prepared to be labelled cold, dull and inadequate.

Other traps beckon in examination papers where pupils are asked to 'discuss', say, the outcome of a court case in which the judge awarded custody to the child's father, an accountant, rather than to its mother, who was living with a plumber (specimen 1988 GCSE paper: SEG, 1986). It is not explicitly stated that the issue is supposed to be parenting styles, although the marking scheme makes the parameters of the question clear for the examiner. Pupils who might wish to discuss the relevance of class or gender inequalities would not gain any marks: they have to bring to the question a knowledge of the values inherent in home economics, if the question is not to become simply a test of comprehension or, more dangerously, a real question. Within the framework of home economics, pupils (including plumbers' daughters) are not allowed to define for themselves what questions may be asked. If topics could be treated in a genuinely open-ended way, the subject would simply explode.

The point of teaching home economics, other than its preservation at all costs as a school subject, now lies in the emphasis on service. The problem of how to set and mark a cookery paper which pupils from any background could do has been circumvented by switching the emphasis from *how* to cook to *whom* to cook *for*: the interrelationship of needs and services. In order to keep gender out of home economics, questions about whose needs are being serviced by whom have to be suppressed.

Many specimen assignments present pupils with short summaries of a situation which places them as the provider of a service to, for example, a physically handicapped child, or a sibling. They tend to reduce people to stereotypes, asking pupils to make an item to give as a present to a handicapped child as though a child's handicap defines the child; asking them to plan a meal for two retired people, as if suggesting that an age group was enough for pupils to infer various other relevant facts. The end results of these assignments could be marked in a culturally neutral manner only if examiners proposed to ignore the content of pupils' answers and mark communication skills alone. However much they attempt to be open, they cannot ultimately evade the fact that cooking, caring for children and other 'domestic' occupations are cultural activities. The neutrality they strive for is not finally possible, unless anything is allowable, but in an examination with a marking scheme it must be assumed that the examiners' openness stops somewhere. Pupils are expected to deliver an appropriate service, without doubting that there is an appropriate service and without asking why.

The National Criteria forced into syllabuses another variety of superficial freedom, since they prohibited not only gender bias but bias on the grounds of race, religion or culture. Years of complaints of monoculturalism in examination papers had not had much effect, but with the introduction of GCSE the examining boards finally had to clean up their act. Black pupils, especially Afro-Caribbean girls in the 1960s and 1970s, had suffered more than other groups of pupils from the educational harm of home economics. This was partly because they were often allowed less choice in the first place and were steered away from academic courses and into non-examination classes, which for girls would usually include domestic subjects. Their examination choices were also restricted, as one West Indian university student, quoted in an article by Yvonne Collymore (June 1974), reported:

> I was only allowed to take cookery, needlework and religious education as subjects at O-level. I was told that my English was not good enough to take

> English language, and because of timetable difficulties could not take science. The careers officer tried to persuade me to do catering but I went to classes to add further O- and A- levels.

The 'problem', as it was seen, of teaching immigrant pupils in home economics classes had begun to disturb the tranquillity of domestic crafts teaching a few years earlier, and at first the proposed solutions tended to focus on exotic vegetables. Pictures of these on the walls, it was suggested to cookery teachers, would make pupils feel more at home.

Faced with pupils who could not eat pork or beef, some teachers who felt unable to adapt simply gave up and left the profession. Many more saw themselves positively as having a role in the forefront of multiculturalism, helping pupils to link the cultures of home and school. A Schools Council-linked survey in the early 1970s found that the great majority of home economics department heads were in favour of using their subject to prepare pupils for 'life in a multiracial society', although only just over half thought their current syllabuses were adapted to do this in any way. In London a group of home economics teachers set up an informal working party in 1973, to pool multicultural resources and produce teaching aids (Gillett, 1974, p. 139).

The ATDS journal *Housecraft* published a series of articles by Yvonne Collymore in 1974, offering advice on teaching home economics in multicultural schools. Collymore's analysis was much more astute than the solutions she was able to offer, given the rigidity of the subject at the time. She referred directly to racism as the major factor underlying Caribbean pupils' underachievement. Her discussion of immigrant parents' hostility towards home economics teaching is illuminating, and reminiscent of the objections voiced by working-class parents in Britain in the nineteenth century:

> ... parents have the impression that they are not being taught anything in schools. In fact, some parents have the idea that their children are taught these 'non-academic' subjects deliberately to prevent them from studying English, mathematics and science ... Often, the feeling is that lessons such as home economics are designed not so much to produce better housewives and mothers but to provide more domestics for hospitals and canteens, office and factory cleaners, and cooks for cafés and restaurants. (May 1974, pp. 136–7)

Collymore appeared to understand parents' fears and the real experiences of racism and hardship which lay behind them, yet her task was to reconcile parents to home economics teaching, defuse their anxieties and present the subject as a most important channel of communication between home and school. She cited examples of parents invited to meals at school which their daughters had cooked, mothers invited in with their babies for the benefit of parentcraft classes. The school could pass on vital information, since 'bedmaking, washing up, laundry and house-cleaning are carried out quite differently in tropical countries so immigrants to Britain will be unfamiliar with English practices'. Immigrant pupils might not know about blankets, carpets or vacuum cleaners, so it was important to teach about these.

The stress, in her suggestions for adapting the existing syllabus, was on how little teachers needed to change their existing practices. The basic framework of courses which pupils had to follow could remain intact, she reassured teachers, although she stressed the need to respect religious or cultural taboos. It was a question of allowing some pupils a certain individual licence, in exchange for requiring them to work through the normal elements of the curriculum:

> Somewhere during the course of four or five years needlework pupils should have the choice of making a garment traditional to their home culture, even if some of the items made during the course are obligatory. (p. 103)

> Why not allow the West Indian girls to make this version [macaroni-and-cheese] on condition that they learn to make a cheese sauce on another occasion? (p. 66)

It seems less likely that Collymore was setting these limits herself than that she felt it would be unrealistic to expect more. There was an oppressive irony in the approaches which saw home economics teaching as a means to mutual understanding between majority and minority cultures, in a period when it was operating as a vehicle for racism in more than one sense. While – at best – making accommodating gestures such as Yvonne Collymore proposed, it continued to send out its message about the correctness and superiority of a single mode of living: British, white, Gentile, rigidly sex-stereotyped and saturated with the values of the post-war middle class. Furthermore, this teaching was effectively forced on many Afro-Caribbean girls, whilst they and their parents were frustrated in their expectations of a high standard of general education in British schools.

Changes in approaches to multicultural education were reflected especially clearly in home economics, because of the obviously cultural basis of much of its content. A decade after *Housecraft* was considering ways of allowing for pupils' differing backgrounds, religious beliefs and even colour and physiology (for example, encouraging teachers to advise West Indian girls on the most suitable choice of British fashion for their figures and skin type) this model of multicultural education was under attack. The 'problem' of multiracial schools became less amenable to solution for home economics, without a radical reshaping of the curriculum.

Sue Oliver (1984) examined assessment as an area of particular concern, since existing syllabuses, examination papers and methods of assessment were quite clearly unfair to many pupils. Her analysis of the state of the subject drew attention to the culturally specific nature of the criteria for assessment, which privileged one set of methods for practical work alone as 'correct' and relied on pupils' familiarity with a fixed content which was shaped by both race and class bias. According to Oliver, teachers were often unaware how alien the subject appeared to their pupils, especially to Asian girls who made great efforts to learn seemingly arbitrary rules and concepts and prepared dishes they could not eat, which they would then have to throw away *'although the pupils would not disclose this'* (p. 23; original emphasis). The suffering, revulsion and humiliation this phrase covers have to be imagined, together with the power over girls' lives of a school regime which forced them to keep silent.

Evidence of this nature provided an eloquent argument for deeper changes, which would not only allow for cultural variation but would also remove all possible causes of cultural disadvantage. In her conclusions, Sue Oliver called for teachers to adopt an actively anti-racist stance and argued that developing cross-cultural studies in home economics 'could help create positive attitudes towards the expression of cultural variation'.

The problem of finding genuinely multicultural assessment criteria surely provided much of the impetus for the change from content to process which featured so strongly in the new GCSE. The General Criteria for GCSE warned that 'every possible effort must be made to ensure that syllabuses and examinations are free of political, ethnic, gender and other forms of bias' (SEC, 1986b, p. 7). This was asking a lot from a subject which had so recently been requiring girls to practise washing their brothers' shirts or to have a repertoire of 'standard' pastry- and cake-making techniques ready to demonstrate. As with their attempts to exclude gender bias, there is now considerable evidence that examination boards and educational publishers, with critical encouragement from teachers, have recently been attempting to exclude bias on the grounds of race and culture.

Any sample of home economics teaching materials still in use in schools would unquestionably reveal examples of continuing bias. One commentator in the late 1980s who turned up instances of racist and sexist bias from his inspection of a sample of home economics texts included in his advice a recommendation that pupils should stick warnings about racist or sexist content in their textbooks (Antonouris, 1987). Teachers now know that they need to watch out; that books cannot be trusted, although efforts to move away from the old, insular ethnocentricity have even made matters worse in some cases. One textbook referred to earlier (Nuffield Home Economics, 1985a) portrayed two Black women, out of dozens of photographs and other illustrations. One was a mother with a baby strapped on her back, shown in a clearly non-European, agricultural setting (she appeared to be hoeing). The other was a young woman working as a nanny for a white family. The token sprinkling of Black children in the illustrations included a girl whose photograph, next to a section on children dressing up, showed her wearing a Brünnhilde-blonde wig. These images, almost the total non-white representation, can hardly have been chosen at random: they reveal the limits of the editors' and publishers' attempts at inclusiveness.

The multicultural, anti-racist home economics project seems to me as likely to reach its goal as a desert traveller stumbling towards a mirage. Mullard (1985) has described the strategies of trying first to assimilate, then to integrate and finally to include, in a form of cultural pluralism, 'black kids in white schools', as alternative power models. All seek ultimately to protect the interests and the power of dominant white groups. What home economics seeks to protect is itself, its existence. It cannot afford to question too closely the perspectives which it embodies, for fear of its ultimate disintegration.

The favoured recent strategy has been to dump a percentage of its content and embrace process as a bias-free alternative, with the implication that process can be evaluated separately from content, and can be considered neutral. This myth of neutrality conceals the original essentially

Western and colonial construction of the subject, and diverts attention from potential conflict between its own values and any others.

Culture cannot be treated as simply another variable. It comes first; it determines what process is; it sets up value systems which rival the health and efficiency motifs of home economics, even if the rivalry is driven underground. Cultural bias is not to be found simply in a few unreconstructed oversights in textbooks and examinations; it is everywhere. The new emphasis in home economics on delivering appropriate services to designated consumers is as culturally bound as the earlier emphasis on the correct way to serve a Victoria sponge.

In its assumptions about families, about the relationship of the family to the community and about what the community is, as well as in its concentration on the minutiae of domestic life, an entirely culturally specific portrait of the objects of its teaching lies lightly buried. References to the needs of the elderly, for instance, require pupils to deduce certain information: that old people live alone or in small households, in poverty and often in poor health, without much capacity for making autonomous decisions about their lives. The constantly implied need for special services, presented as the means for extracting more specific information and decisions from pupils, is never itself open to question. That the world just has to be a certain way for old people is seen as a fact, external to culture.

In its focus on nutrition, while appearing open to an infinite variety of diets and cookery styles, all are reduced to the same common denominators as if it makes sense to apply the same criteria for improvement to all. Data from national dietary guidelines is extrapolated to make it appear that everyone is in the same danger of heart disease, and in the cause of avoiding bias pupils can work out how to reduce the fat content in samosas instead of Cornish pasties, as if their different dietary contexts are irrelevant. Rather than simply including 'ethnic' foods, home economics sets out to evaluate, criticise and alter them. It allows itself to do this because the criteria are, after all, supposedly neutral: it does not see that such goals as eating less fat are themselves related to specific groups rather than to the entire world.

Reducing people's lives to common denominators and to a series of sensible choices, home economics forgets or ignores the other codes for living which already exist. Girls may no longer be compelled to cook foods they are unable to eat and would prefer not to touch, but they are still being guided into a system of rules for decision-taking about home and family life. Their own rules may be recognised as exceptions in class, although only when they become visible. The existence of alternative, preferred and self-contained systems cannot be made visible, recognised or sanctioned. Acknowledging the overriding importance of their own codes would call into question the very point and purpose of the work.

One day during Ramadan a home economics class started a value-for-money survey of some different branded foodstuffs. Some of the girls were fasting, and they were not made to take part in the taste-comparison test. The girls who were fasting would have known already which foods they could choose and which they could not. This knowledge is not something which can be subsumed under other information; it made the test redundant for them. The teacher was reminded about Ramadan, but had no way of noticing the irrelevance of the lesson for some of the members of her class.

It does not require a strong framework of religious rules or customs, or an easily identifiable non-British culture, for pupils to have their own system of knowledge and decision-making already in place. Pupils who know explicitly about their own codes may even find conflicts easier to manage than those whose code is implicit, like the girl from a white English family who told me, with reference to the shopping survey, that 'you just go to wherever you go'. The Asian girls Sue Oliver referred to, who had to make brown stew, simply threw the food away afterwards. It may be harder to throw away a more subtle form of cultural domination, which presents pupils with implied rules they are not going to adopt but still leaves behind the message that the way they have always done things is irrational, mindless or wrong.

Teachers are often aware that pupils do not come to school devoid of skills or resources, or wanting to discard their own perspectives in favour of something new. One particularly sensitive teacher explained that home economics lessons offered the chance to value what pupils brought in with them. It is likely that many other teachers share this view in respect of some, although not usually all, of their pupils. This raises the question of why the purpose of school should become, in this instance, valuing what pupils already know rather than offering them opportunities to learn more. Should pupils in this situation feel pleased that their knowledge from home is being validated for 10 per cent of their time in school, or angry that their time is being wasted?

The clash between a committed culture and the home economics commitment to avoid bias and present itself as neutral, culture-free, is also a struggle for power between school and home. It can have different outcomes, depending on the relative power and homogeneity of pupils' parent cultures in any one setting. George Riseborough (1988) described an extraordinary near-reversal of the situation in mainstream schools in his study of a non-Jewish home economics teacher working in a Jewish school, who had to rely on pupils' information and knowledge and obtained the trust of parents and staff by adhering to their codes of practice rather than her own. Riseborough's discussion was curiously limited by his own aims: he was interested in the position of teacher as worker subjected to outside forces, in showing that neutral education does not exist and that child-centred education need not necessarily be radical. His tale, he argued, 'by *familiarising* us with a very *unfamiliar* world ... has the power to *defamiliarise* the more general, taken-for-granted, non-Jewish world of *Anybody*' (p. 50).

I read the tale another way, since it describes to me a familiar world where the rules would not be as alien as they would be in the home economics room of a standard British school. The power which had apparently passed from teacher to pupils and parents was the power to determine what Riseborough termed 'recipe knowledge', around which the teacher's lessons revolved. Riseborough took for granted this pattern of home economics teaching, yet the greatest change in home economics recently has been precisely the move away from 'recipe knowledge', which is so obviously cultural knowledge. The reversal he describes not only could not happen in most other schools, but as home economics is currently constructed it could hardly happen anywhere now. The process-orientated version reinstates all teachers as experts. Content could sometimes have been subject to negotiation, as in Riseborough's case-study; process is not.

Home economics teaching for pupils over sixteen, and some fourteen-to-sixteen-year-olds, has recently fragmented into a variety of courses. In the 1980s the old craft skills teaching and the new orientation towards service, which fitted in well with a government philosophy of returning to 'care in the community' (usually meaning by women, unpaid), met and meshed with the 'new vocationalism'. While the titles were new, the contents of these courses supposedly designed to equip pupils, particularly those who would otherwise add to the rising total of youth unemployment, with marketable skills were a familiar combination of domestic skills teaching coupled with the rhetoric of 'service'. The schedule for one Certificate of Pre-Vocational Education (CPVE) 'services to people' course even listed housewife, nanny and mother's help amongst the occupational roles it was geared towards – revealing evidence of how substantially similar the aims of some course providers were to those of their nineteenth-century counterparts.

Millman (1985) found that the Technical and Vocational Education Initiative (TVEI) was not in fact providing girls with equal opportunities, in spite of an avowed intention to do so; girls were still concentrated within traditionally female subject areas, 'training' for work which was an extension of the domestic, caring role within the home. Skeggs (1988) noted that girls on 'caring'-type courses were often critical of the course content, but although they expressed scorn for activities such as bathing dolls – 'that doll crap' – they appeared to be affected by the course emphasis on secure family life, and its link with efficiency in child-rearing and home-making practices. Skeggs described such courses as virtually 'domestic apprenticeships', more effective in socialising girls away from the labour market than in preparing them for it.

The 1988 Education Reform Act presented home economics teachers with their most serious threat to date. The national curriculum, a combination of grammar school nostalgia and hard-headedness, not surprisingly had no room for the new incarnation of home economics. NATHE, as well as many teachers, began to pin their hopes on the two fundamental craft skills within home economics finding a logical home as components of design and technology. As one former NATHE president wrote, 'There is no single established subject which is said to be 'technology' and perhaps it is in this area that home economics can be said to be a foundation subject' (Yorke, 1988).

After the plethora of material explaining why any study of food or textiles had to be linked to home and family, the recommendations of the National Curriculum Design and Technology Working Group (1988) are like a breath of fresh air. The inclusion of the food and textiles branches of home economics was influenced by a perceived need to make design and technology more 'girl-friendly' – at least as much as by NATHE and their supporters, who welcomed the interim report (NATHE, 1989). Margaret Yorke, quoted above, had argued that girls would view science and technology more positively if they were linked to human needs, and that this could be done by integrating them with home economics (assumptions which are discussed more fully in Chapter 5 of this book). Girls would then feel at home in the science laboratory, and boys in the home economics room.

The implications for home economics of becoming a sub-section of design and technology are considerable, and affect both pupils and teachers. There is still a danger that the implementation of this aspect of the national curriculum will lead to more girls doing more cooking and sewing, although the working party issued a clear warning against allowing pupils to narrow the focus of their work to a domestic context. The emphasis on design at least gives pupils the possibility of working with food in ways seldom allowed before within home economics, where they have frequently been expected simply to follow instructions, or to produce dishes from a restricted repertoire.

The long-standing problem of status, as I argue in the next chapter, continues to absorb home economics teachers. Virtually all women, they would in all probability find that the integration of their subject with CDT, taught overwhelmingly by men who have a tendency to hold somewhat traditional views (Grant, 1983; Spear, 1985) presents them with new status problems. A further anxiety could be the uncertain future of other areas of home economics teaching if practical work became the province of design and technology.

The creators of GCSE Home Economics tried to deflect attention from the ideological core of their subject by concentrating on process rather than content, but the newer insistence on content appears to have called their bluff. Without the glue of gender, the claim that home economics constitutes a unified field of study may finally become impossible to sustain. The doctrine of separate spheres on which home economics ultimately rests has not disappeared, but in a rare positive sign for education it has not been enshrined in the national curriculum. It is now more apparent than ever that anything useful in home economics lies in areas which could be covered by other subjects with more depth and with more possibilities of an openly critical approach.

4

On the Margins: Status Matters

One day in 1988 I had a telephone conversation with a man who told me, with great emphasis, that he was personally in charge of authorising all visits to schools, for all subjects and for any purpose whatsoever. No researcher could visit a school in his local education authority without clearance from him. I then explained that I wanted to observe home economics lessons, and immediately his manner changed; he lost all interest in me. I was so struck by what he said next that I wrote it down: 'I deal with everything except home economics. I don't know anything about that at all. Come to think of it, I don't even know who does.'

No other incident did more to confirm for me that status was a key issue for home economics teachers. About the first thing I noticed about home economics teachers in staff rooms – where they appeared less often than other teachers anyway – was their separateness, years before I knew anything of the reasons. This chapter looks at what this separate, usually low status has meant for teachers. They seem to have been forever caught between two fears: the fear of marginalisation if they remain as they are, complete with low status and a feminine identity, and the fear of annihilation if they dare to change too much.

Teachers told me bitter stories of exclusion, contempt and injustice. They were aware of being shown less respect as teachers by some of their colleagues than they deserved. One head teacher expected home economics staff to take responsibility for her morning cup of tea; in another school senior staff had timetabled a streamed group of less academic boys to take home economics 'as a joke'.

Conditions of work for home economics staff were visibly worse than for other teachers. They had less time to visit the staff room because lessons so often overran, their teaching rooms were usually housed away from the main part of the school (often in a separate block shared with other practical departments) and their ancillary help was insufficient. In the lunch break they often had to shop for essential ingredients. Their complaints went right back to their years at training college, where some teachers felt they had been made to work harder than other students and allowed less free time on their timetables, besides always being singled out as different. One teacher spoke with heavy irony of her mother's advice, which had in all innocence duped her into a disappointing career: 'Be a cookery teacher, that's a good job for a woman.' Another gestured around her and said, 'I teach in a kitchen.'

Women in home economics have had to fight their corner for a long time. A contradictory portrait of the women involved in home economics teaching emerges from any account of the subject's history. They were traditionalists almost by definition, especially in their views about women's role, but in the early years they were also pioneers. Organising for a domestic feminism, they were militants at least for their own cause. Within the teaching profession they can claim more than most groups of teachers to have a history of their own, differentiated from the general profession by their distinctive status and a century of separate training.

Training for teachers of domestic subjects began in the same way as domestic economy teaching in schools, developing gradually through the influence of some scattered voluntary organisations. Official recognition was slow, and funds were scarce. Yoxall (1913, p.10) reports a story that water dripped through the roof of the National Training School's first premises into the pupils' frying pans, and the college had to use money earned from its catering operations to build itself a better home. Both the public elementary-school system itself and the mainstream network of training colleges in Britain which grew up to service it were founded on the efforts of voluntary organisations, but they at least had the resources of the Church of England or of the Nonconformist churches behind them, as well as some state support. The colleges which trained teachers of domestic subjects were set up outside this system, and remained somewhat apart from the mainstream for a hundred years.

Specialist training colleges for domestic subjects teachers started out as 'Schools of Cookery', the first of which was the 'National Training School of Cookery', founded in 1873. From 1874 onwards other Schools were opened in Leeds, Liverpool and elsewhere, until by 1894 there were seventeen specialist training colleges (Yoxall, 1913). The Schools did not at first train teachers at all. Their earliest pupils were middle-class women, who attended lectures and demonstrations on cookery. The idea was that they would teach cookery to working-class women too, but the latter showed scant interest, and so eventually a different idea took hold – that teachers should be trained to spread the work of the Schools further. The training colleges were set up for women, although a sea-cook was sent to the National for training as a teacher before setting up classes in cookery at the Sailors' Home, London Docks. Other Nautical Schools of Cookery for boys wanting to be sea-cooks were opened in Liverpool and a few more seaport towns.

The Education Department began to recognise the work of the training schools from 1893, when it issued its own regulations for them (Dent, 1977, p. 40), but 'did not offer the normal teacher-training grant, but only the much smaller grant for technical courses. This injustice was not rectified until 1906; before then, several Schools of Cookery had been forced by shortage of funds to give up training teachers.'

When the Schools of Cookery – which also taught other subjects such as laundrywork, domestic economy or 'housewifery' and needlework – were at last given a full teacher training grant in 1907, conditions were attached. The Schools were inspected by the Women's Branch of HM Inspectorate, and as a result of this enquiry's findings were told to enrol trainee teachers separately from other students and make their instruction more efficient (Dent, 1977, pp. 75–6). They were also required to pay more attention to general science. This was followed by an inspection, in 1912 and 1913, of the fourteen recognised Schools. The Inspectors called for a thorough overhaul of the Schools' work, not because it was considered bad but because it was so different from the training in the general colleges.

Among the Inspectors' criticisms were that 'the "Special" subjects were not correlated with the general science' and that 'the subject matter taught had little relevance to the homes from which Elementary school children came'. From 1915, instead of taking separate 'Special subjects' courses, all students recognised for grant had to take a two-year combined course.

There are nearly a hundred photographs taken in domestic science colleges among the illustrations in Cassell's *Household Guide*, a six-volume manual for middle-class women which was published in 1911. The

women in them were mostly teachers or students at the National Society's Training College or at the Northfield School of Domestic Science,
which was in the north London district of Stamford Hill. They are
shown demonstrating various operations in cookery and laundrywork,
which if they were included in the courses for teachers in training would
certainly have substantiated the Inspectors' criticisms about the irrelevance for elementary-school children of much of the work.

In the long dresses of the time, and usually wearing the neat white caps
and full aprons which were recommended for respectable servants,
women from domestic economy training colleges stand dishing up quails
on toast, glazing galantine of fowl or arranging prawns and shrimps in
the chopped aspic border of a mayonnaise of turbot. Four photographs
show a teacher or student demonstrating different folds for serviettes.
Captions under the laundrywork photographs speak of the earnest
delight to be found in its chores from washing to goffering. 'It takes
several years to arouse enthusiasm for the dolly-tub, but once the con-
quest is made it holds good for a lifetime'; 'The double process of
sprinkling and folding is an art in itself.' The largest photograph shows
'The Mending Class in the National Society's Training College for
Teachers of Domestic Economy'. Twelve women in caps and aprons sit
round tables bent over their work, while a teacher hovers nearby.

At first the two-year courses the domestic economy colleges offered
were fairly comparable with the two-year course which used to be standard in general colleges. Domestic economy formed an element of the
curriculum in the general colleges which trained women as elementary-
school teachers, and its inclusion was arguably a factor in deterring
middle-class women from entering the profession (Widdowson, 1980,
pp. 47–8). It featured partly because women were thought to need some
training in order to manage their own domestic lives whilst employed
as schoolmistresses (the publication by the Education Union of a
domestic manual, *How a schoolmistress may live upon seventy pounds a year*,
also provides evidence of a belief that women teachers needed to learn
thrifty management on their low incomes) and partly because women
in elementary schools were expected to teach a modicum of domestic
subjects anyway. A third reason was that the work required of student
teachers helped to keep down the domestic costs of the colleges
themselves.

The fact that non-specialist teachers were expected to teach needlework, as it was included in their general training, prevented the specialist colleges from gaining recognition for the needlework certificates they awarded. Ailsa Yoxall argued that needlework teaching was in an unsatisfactory state because of this:

> ... the Board of Education does not require the services of specially-qualified teachers for this subject, as it is included in the regular training for certificated women-teachers in Training Colleges, where it is not feasible to allow sufficient time for it. (Yoxall, 1913, p. 20)

While some graduate teachers were also being trained in colleges and university departments for secondary-school teaching in particular, and to a much smaller extent for elementary (later primary) teaching, domestic subjects teaching remained firmly a non-graduate profession until fairly recent times, when teacher training was reorganised in the 1970s.

Various accounts of the history of teacher training for domestic subjects (Yoxall, 1913; Weddell, 1955; Dent, 1977) refer to the shortage of students, as an almost constant theme. The domestic colleges never appear to have had the same attraction as the general colleges, which offered the main route into higher education for many women whether or not they actually wished to teach. The marriage bar which operated between the wars may also have proved a greater deterrent to women holding a more traditional and less academic outlook, as well as driving women out of their jobs. The ban on married women teachers was ended in 1944 – as David describes (1980, p. 161), it was seen by its critics as the 'height of irony' for women with children to be excluded from teaching, and the irony was of course more acute when the very subjects they taught were concerned with domestic work and the care of children.

The separate existence of the training colleges meant that their standards were criticised as lower and different, but after reorganisation students still faced the realisation that they were not taken as seriously as others, or offered equal treatment. As late as the 1980s a former home economics student complained that she had been 'teased' at college by fellow students asking her to wash their shirts.

As well as their own colleges, teachers of domestic subjects had their own union within a union. The Association of Teachers of Domestic Science (ATDS) was formed in 1896, originally attached to the National

Union of Women Workers and latterly to the NUT. Between 1909 and 1962 its initials stood for 'Association of Teachers of Domestic Subjects'; in 1962 'subjects' was changed back to 'science', until 1983 when it changed its name to the National Association of Teachers of Home Economics (NATHE). The Association campaigned against the low status of domestic subjects in a variety of ways: trying to gain more space for them in secondary schools, persuade the universities to take them seriously, and generally to improve their academic image. They had occasional successes.

In 1910 Alice Ravenhill and Catherine Schiff published a collection of essays entitled *Household administration: its place in the higher education of women*. The contributing authors set out to establish a case for teaching domestic science as an academic subject at university level. Wenona Hoskyns-Abrahall, for example, in a chapter on 'The place of biology in the equipment of women', argued that if housewives were taught bacteriology they would be able to ensure cleaner and more hygienic homes – hardly the argument to win support from other lobbyists for women's entrance to higher education. In their preface, Ravenhill and Schiff widened the argument:

> ... blind instinct must yield place to trained intelligence if home life is to be preserved and modern conditions of existence adequately adjusted to human requirements ... In order that desirable saving in time, money, labour, health or happiness shall be effected, graduate women of high attainments are urgently needed for the work. It is they only who can bring to bear upon the problems of childhood and adolescence, of food, of clothing, of housing, of domestic economics, of occupation, of rest and recreation, the patient study and research in the interests of humanity, which men of similar standing have lavished upon the advancement of commerce and industrial processes. It is by their skilled labour in the almost untrodden field of domestic science that the millions of homes will benefit which are committed to the charge of women who possess neither time, opportunity, nor ability to carry out these indispensable investigations ...

The vision of a vanguard of graduates in domestic science conducting research into improved methods of household management was partially fulfilled when King's College for Women in London initiated a course in 'Household Science'. Sheffield University recognised domestic science as a university subject in 1911, to the extent of allowing students to take the science part of their course at the University and the domestic part at the Sheffield Training College. Battersea Polytechnic offered a diploma in science as applied to housecraft from the 1890s, and at the University College of Wales short non-teaching courses in the theory and practice of domestic science were arranged for women students.

Much later the vision has remained essentially the same, but home economists have never managed to achieve the academic standing for their subject which they would wish it to have. At degree and postgraduate level, home economics still barely has a toehold in the universities and is taught by few of the polytechnics and institutes of higher education. Despite the supposed equivalence between polytechnic and university degrees, the lack of university teaching of their subject is certainly seen as undermining by home economics practitioners. A revealing article by Brenda Pratt (1986) on research in home economics referred to anxieties about academic status. She suggested that home economics researchers tend not to be involved in pushing back frontiers of knowledge at all, leaving it to other professions to bring about changes in thinking. According to Pratt, home economics already had two of the three elements of academic respectability, a research journal and a research conference. 'The third element, a standard undergraduate text-book, does not exist.'

The 'academic respectability' of home economics, about which Pratt was so explicitly concerned, was not enhanced by what she described as 'the real problem within the subject, namely the apparent response of the subject to external criticism rather than through 'internal' debate of critical issues'. The example she gave was the connection between home economics and nutrition:

> The present criticism from outside the subject of the emphasis within school courses on traditional cookery skills would not have occurred if the issue of the relationship between cooking and diet had been raised and resolved within the home economics community as a whole.

This amounted to an extraordinary confession that the home economics community did not especially think about cookery in terms of diet and health until outsiders – in this case health education personnel – pointed out the connection to them. Pratt's main concern appeared to be that this did their own practitioners, teachers and researchers no good at all, in terms of academic respectability. Such work ought to have been done by home economics researchers, she argued, although her only explana-

tion of why they had avoided it was that for som...
pose of undertaking research was to meet th...
institutions. Yet in raising the question of why home...
rather than leads, it is virtually answered: the article s...
self-confidence from beginning to end, of a subject whic...
feel its status secure enough to begin taking risks.

The marked absence of home economics from the univer... ...o
long is a story of continuing failure for its supporters, for they ...tainly
tried hard to persuade the academic establishment to their cause. The
ATDS archive includes correspondence from a campaign in the late
1950s and early 1960s, aimed at increasing the number of relevant
courses in higher education. In 1959 the ATDS Secretary, Angela
Crawley, submitted a memorandum to each university which had one
domestic science training college, or more, in its area. The ATDS begged
to submit to the universities its opinion that the time was now propitious
for the institution of additional degree courses, and asked them to consider setting up degree courses in domestic science. The memorandum
referred to a growing awareness amongst domestic scientists that they
were in need of workers in their subject who had studied the different
aspects of their work at university level.

These overtures were brushed off with varying degrees of courtesy.
Bristol University pointed out one relevant course which it already offered. Most replies were merely formal acknowledgements, but others
reeked of male scorn. The most superficially sympathetic reply was also
the most derisive, the university registrar concerned writing that he
thought it a good idea and the matter would be placed on the agenda,
but he knew what would be said by the various departmental heads,
who were quite clear that 'science' meant physics and engineering. This
correspondence bears witness to more than a failed attempt by a subject
seen as trivial to gain respect from the academic establishment. I also read
it as painful proof of the relative powerlessness of a women's organisation compared with the might of the men who planned and controlled
the higher levels of learning.

The ATDS continued its efforts to increase the number of courses
available in higher education when in 1961 it issued a memorandum of
evidence to the Committee on Higher Education. Many of the points
made in this document reflected a view of the status quo, in terms of
girls' educational and career aspirations and the role of women in the

e and in society, as unproblematic and unlikely to change. It noted that fewer girls than boys were interested in non-vocational higher education while they tended to have an earlier preoccupation and interest in marriage, and presented this as an argument for making more domestic science courses at the post-secondary level available. The memorandum stated that there were only two universities currently offering degree courses or opportunities for research in any aspect of domestic science, and pleaded for the granting of a first degree course in domestic science as such. It expressed concern that social science courses, then an expanding area, were not set up in co-operation with domestic science courses.

The document is most reminiscent of John Newsom's anti-feminist polemic *The Education of Girls* (1948) in its paragraph on the 'needs' of girls studying other courses at universities or colleges other than domestic science colleges, whom it claimed should make some study of domestic science to increase their knowledge and efficiency as home-makers, and enable them to make a more valuable contribution to society. Sixth form colleges and A levels ought to be replanned in this respect. These proposals, which would have delighted Newsom, would have moved the feminists who strove to gain entry for women into higher education to despairing protest. The document exemplifies the paradox of 'domestic feminism': in making apparently progressive points about domestic science as a core subject in liberal higher education, and about the need for university-level scientific and technological research in their field, the authors were also promoting the most oppressively traditional ideas about gender roles and restating the old theme, elaborated by Ravenhill and Schiff, that women in higher education should study ways of becoming better housewives.

The credibility of A level home economics was another area of struggle between the ATDS and the universities. It did not have equal status with other subjects and was often not recognised or accepted as an entry qualification for courses in higher education. In this area too the Association made repeated efforts to change perceptions of their subject's status, conducting a survey of A level teaching in 1969 with the aim of proving its worth and importance. An ATDS leaflet published in 1976 formed part of another publicity campaign, setting out the current situation together with the recommendation that A level home economics should be an acceptable subject for entry to all establishments of higher educa-

approach with a tendency to be female orientated and white middle class in its ethos' (Boult and Gull, 1989, p. 90), which were limiting its advancement towards the general academic acceptability it has still not achieved.

In schools, there were two main grounds on which home economics had to fight to try to shake off its low-grade image: over the curriculum for older, more academic and usually middle-class girls, and over the hierarchical division of subjects which so often accompanied a system of streaming pupils. The oldest and fiercest campaign centred on the place of domestic education in the new girls' secondary schools in the late nineteenth and early twentieth centuries.

The domestic economy pioneers had their feminist counterparts in the campaigners who were trying to gain access for women to higher education, and setting up secondary schools for middle-class girls which aimed to provide an academic education equivalent to that available for boys. The two movements had a little common ground (Marion Bidder, who taught at Newnham and Girton colleges in Cambridge, collaborated with Florence Baddeley of the Gloucestershire School of Cookery and Domestic Economy in the production of one textbook for student teachers) but the main area of conflict was over the place of domestic subjects in the secondary curriculum. The head teachers of the new girls' schools generally tried to keep them out as far as possible, while the domestic subjects' teachers and their supporters wanted to establish that girls of all classes and all levels of ability needed some form of teaching for the domestic duties which would surely befall them one day.

There was much passion on both sides. The headmistress Dorothea Beale replied as follows to the criticisms of a Miss Sewell:

> ... I must regret that Miss Sewell repeats the popular cry that women are to be 'educated for the home' by learning 'cookery and needlework and arithmetic enough for accounts'. These home arts are easily acquired by those whose minds are well trained, and the place for them to be learned is home, though they may and should be encouraged at school. But can it possibly be thought that such things can compare in importance with studies to which Miss Sewell does not even allude – elementary physiology and the laws of health – and those which open the eyes to see the wonders of the material

Dorothea Beale was still obliged to use the defence that studying classics and mathematics would help a mother 'to take an interest in the work of schoolboy sons'; in 1888, the year her article was published, it was scarcely possible to defend the right of even a middle-class girl's intellectual education in terms of her own interests. Girls' secondary schools also continued the tradition of including needlework as an indispensable item in the curriculum, its acceptability as a genteel lady's occupation compensating for its status as a domestic subject. In spite of the constraints she was under, a glimpse of the seriousness of the fight and the hostility felt by one camp for another breaks through Dorothea Beale's carefully controlled language when she compares 'such things' as the elements of domestic economy to the elements of a scientific education. There is no doubt that the domestic economy reformers, for their part, recognised and resented the contempt her words implied, and fought back.

In the early years a few secondary schools did offer classes in cookery and other domestic subjects. 'In other schools', Ailsa Yoxall wrote crossly,

> ... where the ideal was purely intellectual, backward girls only were instructed in the domestic arts – a state of things which needs little comment; for however much the girls as individuals might benefit by their home training, the whole principle of it was wrong and based on the fallacy that neither special aptitude nor much brain-power is necessary for a good housewife – the only career open to a dull girl. (p. 47).

Yoxall also criticised girls' secondary schools for seeing domestic subjects, apart from needlework, as outside the ordinary curriculum, and for allocating too little time to them when they were included. When the reason was not prejudice, she suggested that it was because timetables were already overcrowded with examination subjects which were wrongly regarded as essential. She pinned her hopes on hygiene, as a branch of home economics, displacing from girls' education other unspecified subjects which, she implied, could not be as important:

> ... the growing sense of the national importance of hygiene in its widest meaning will overcome this difficulty in the near future, even if it necessitates the abandonment of some subjects now considered indispensable.

Emphasising hygiene was one way of securing acceptance for domestic economy teaching in the secondary schools, but the strategy most of the subject's supporters eventually chose to adopt was to link it with science teaching for girls (Yoxall stressed her approval for joint domestic economy and science schemes of work) or else to present it as a science in itself: domestic science. Women who had forged careers for themselves as pioneers of domestic education were in the forefront of the campaign to gain recognition for domestic science: Florence Baddeley (Principal of the Gloucestershire School of Cookery), Alice Ravenhill, Catherine Schiff, and Catherine Buckton of the Leeds School Board, whose own books tended towards teaching 'hygiene' as the most essential element of domestic science.

The move towards redefining domestic economy as domestic science was international, and was particularly successful in America (Ehrenreich and English, 1979). One of its successes in Britain was the introduction of the course in household science for women at King's College, previously mentioned. Other ventures, like the ATDS proposal of 1911 to link science teaching in girls' schools with domestic science throughout the secondary years, met with less success. This plan, and the continuing presentation of domestic economy and latterly home economics as versions of science for girls, are discussed more fully in a later chapter.

The success of many girls' grammar schools in keeping home economics out was still frustrating the ATDS far into the twentieth century. A report the Association commissioned showed that in the late 1960s girls in single-sex schools were less likely than girls in mixed schools to study domestic science in their first two years of secondary education. Its author found this surprising and a cause for concern:

> ... it could be that in girls' schools the value of the part played by practical subjects in the natural development of the pupil is not recognised ... It is unfortunate that a subject which is of importance to all girls is often excluded from the career-based courses and this is particularly the case in girls' grammar schools ... (ATDS, 1967, p. 105)

The report concluded that *all* girls of *all* abilities should be given what it termed adequate opportunity to study domestic science.

Throughout all these attempts to make some form of home economics education compulsory for women undergraduates, sixth-formers or grammar school girls, there was strangely little evidence of a demand, let alone a need, for such teaching from any quarter except the home economics community itself. Compared with the strength of the arguments about inadequate working-class homes, it seemed that there was little to say about the inadequacy of middle-class homes or of untrained graduate mothers. The case for extending the scope of home economics was not made on the basis of any such need, real or not, but was predicated on the belief that the low status of the subject derived from its association with lower-class, lower-ability pupils.

The difficulty for teachers resisting the image of home economics as a subject best suited to non-academic pupils has been that at least such a labelling guaranteed them a fairly substantial captive population. Some teachers argued that attempts to make home economics more academic were made at the expense of the majority of pupils studying it, who were confronted with an increasing quantity of written work which might be beyond their capabilities, while they had less time for the practical work which was of more value to them. An anonymous correspondent to *Housecraft* in 1975 thought this was why home economics teachers were leaving the profession in significant numbers (the journal had asked readers to write in with their suggestions as to why this was happening). Although CSE examinations had been intended for the top 60 per cent, she pointed out that teachers faced the problem of trying to teach a subject which had become increasingly academic to the 'bottom 60 per cent' (*Housecraft*, 1975, p. 100).

After the introduction of GCSE, and amidst the outburst of articles emphasising the advanced scientific and technological aspects of home economics which should see it included in the national curriculum, Jane Dimock broke ranks to put forward an updated argument about the conflict between the search for academic status and the needs of actual pupils:

> For several years we have all strived; teachers, inspectors, advisers, to achieve academic recognition for our subject ... All these contribute much to the progress of the child but these efforts have also been intended to promote Home Economics as a subject suitable for more able children. (Dimock, 1989, p. 111)

She argued that the appeal of home economics to less academic children, who might have difficulty coping with the demands of written work, especially for GCSE, had been widely ignored, 'often quite deliberately': 'We all know why – not for the sake of our pupils but for the benefit of our subject.' Her suggestion that home economics ought to return to concentrating on the product, on things pupils could enjoy making and could take home with them as tangible achievements, had a heretical air at a time when other teachers were complaining that they still had to fend off the question 'What are you making?' and explain that it was no longer relevant.

Another article juxtaposed with hers, on textile studies in New South Wales, reflected the current orthodoxy in its conclusion that professionally ambitious and intellectually capable students 'would greatly benefit from participation' in the subject areas of textiles and design and home science, which tended not to attract them (Fritz, 1989, p. 111). The question Dimock raised of who benefits, who loses from the quest for status, must also be asked about reactions to the next transformation for home economics if the national curriculum leads, via technology, to a reassertion of craft skills. Departments were already 'reticent', as she described it, in their attitudes towards the type of unashamedly practical vocational courses offered within TVEI.

One remedy for the problem of low status, to which the home economics community has returned at intervals, is to rename itself and attempt to shed the old prejudices along with the old name. The latest renaming has already been seen as a liability. As recently as 1985, an article by a lecturer at Queen's College, Glasgow, complaining that the course title for a BA in home economics was deterring prospective students, appeared under the heading 'Time for a change of name?' (Campbell, 1985). Yet 'home economics' was meant to improve the image of the subject, as were the names which it replaced. The image persists in catching up.

The ATDS plunged itself into some controversy about new names in the early 1960s when its Secretary, Angela Crawley, wrote officially to the Ministry of Education to convey the Association's deep concern about the choice of name for the subjects which they taught in schools and colleges. The ATDS was worried about the confusion of different names then current. In an exchange of letters which are preserved in the ATDS archive the President, Miss M.E. Robertson, and Angela Crawley commented on a pamphlet called 'Teaching home economics' produced by the principals of the domestic subjects training colleges (as they were then called). They were concerned that it managed to confuse the reader, and did their image no good, by referring to housecraft, domestic subjects and home economics, without explanation.

The ATDS changed its own name in 1962 after nearly three years of discussion, dropping 'Domestic Subjects' in favour of 'Domestic Science'. The membership had argued over numerous variants before finally going back to 'Domestic Science', a name which did not satisfy everyone involved in the debate by any means. Writing from County Hall, Miss D.E. Blackmore, a member of the ATDS, agreed that the change of name was a matter of paramount importance but wanted 'Home Science'.

The intensity of members' feelings over the issue was extraordinary given that 'home science' is simply a modern version of 'domestic science', just as 'home economics' is only another way of saying 'domestic economy': no changes of meaning were involved. The eventual winner, 'Home Economics', is the name given to the subject internationally, the point which proved conclusive. The Association's 1983 name change was part of a renewed campaign of promotion for the subject which involved also changing the name of its journal from 'Housecraft' to the mystifying but non-stereotyped title 'Modus'. The new association set out to work more closely with industry and commerce, and the new journal expanded its features section and started to give more space to science (Higgins, 1985).

Changing the name of an institution, a place, a condition or a course in order to improve an image rarely has anything but a short-term effect. Even if bad memories do not linger on, the same attributes which made it formerly unattractive or liable to be disparaged are likely to set off once more the process of investing a name with negative associations. In twentieth-century Britain, 'economics' and 'science' are not words with low-status associations. 'Domestic' and 'home', on the other hand, are – when used as adjectives they imply that what they describe is amateurish, small-scale, tamed, essentially limited. They also signify 'female' rather than 'male'. As long as the focus of home economics is on the home and family, there is little its supporters can do to improve its image by varying its name. As long as the subject exists, they will need to continue to try.

The complaint that home economics is not taken seriously enough – is belittled, marginalised, seen as low-status – is a constant theme in the letters and editorial pages of *Housecraft* and its successor, *Modus*. The overall effect of reading the literature is of witnessing an endless struggle to assert the same virtues in the teeth of the same old prejudices. Home economics' continued failure to establish its academic respectability is much more than an irritation for teachers: it has affected their working conditions and career prospects.

The specific grievances most often mentioned by home economics teachers as the product of their subject's low status are lack of promotion, lack of ancillary help, lack of recognition that they possess specific teaching skills, and the expectation that they will provide the necessary domestic labour for school functions even when these have no connection with their teaching duties. They have been treated for years as tea ladies.

A recent President of NATHE, Margaret Yorke, referred to the failure of home economics teachers to achieve promotion in her inaugural speech:

> If I may reflect back to the AGM of 1957 and quote from the report in *Housecraft*. 'Miss Robertson complained that few headships and deputy headships went to Domestic Science teachers'. That was thirty years ago. Have times changed? How many heads are female, let alone Home Economics trained? (Yorke, 1987, p. 241)

Not only are home economics teachers not promoted to headships, but they complain that they are not given posts of responsibility and are on lower gradings, heads of domestic science departments often ranking a scale lower than heads of other departments. When home economics teachers and CDT staff are joined in a single department, it is the (male) CDT specialist who will usually be appointed to head it.

As long ago as 1956 the ATDS put forward proposals for improved in-service training for its members to equip them for posts of greater responsibility in schools, and tried constantly to make the point that home economists were ideally suited to many senior posts because of the 'breadth' of their training and experience. Home economics teachers clearly were – and are – doubly disadvantaged, as women and as teachers of a 'female' low-status subject.

The few men in home economics do not appear to suffer in this way at all. Their situation compares with that of men in infant and nursery teaching, where women overwhelmingly predominate and men who enter the field are statistically very likely to achieve headships. In home economics, men are likely to achieve the largest salaries and the highest status possible, which means that they are not even to be found in schools but as heads of departments in colleges and polytechnics.

Until the reorganisation of teacher training following the James Report (1972) women were at least guaranteed a certain number of positions as principals of training colleges. The change which began in the mid seventies was quite marked, as one correspondent to *Housecraft* wrote in 1976: 'At least six [domestic science training colleges] now have male principals, which until recently and for many years in the past had been very ably controlled by outstanding women.'

The current situation shows a very large, and unsurprising, discrepancy between the proportion of women to men teaching home economics in schools and the proportion in institutes of higher and further education. Virtually all home economics teachers in schools are women (Arnot, 1984, p. 43), with no serious likelihood of much change having occurred in the last few years. In further and higher education institutions, there are one or two men to every three women acting as heads of home economics departments or their equivalents, from the evidence of names given in the NATHE courses guides (1987, 1988). When the figures for higher education departments are separated from those for further education the inequality is even more apparent, with almost as many men as women heading courses linked to home economics. There has not been an equivalent movement of women into posts usually held by men: women are not suddenly heading half the engineering or physics departments. This is surely one of the most extreme and ironic examples of legislation for sex equality working in favour of men.

While science teachers can assume that they will have ancillary help – laboratory assistants to set up equipment for experiments, help with clearing up, stock control and other essential non-teaching duties – home economics teachers have often been expected to manage with a minimum of assistance, or even none. As they have repeatedly complained, they have at least as great a burden of work to fit in between lessons as have science staff.

Amongst all the complaints I heard or read from home economics teachers about this particular injustice, it did not appear that either as individuals or in an organised way they had fought hard against it, although some mentioned it as another reason to leave the profession.

My impression was that in the past they have tended to cope either by shouldering the added burden of work and complaining only to each other, or by using female pupils as unpaid helpers. If this is so it indicates a degree of acceptance of the situation, also evident in the practice which continued for so long of acting as unofficial caterers, which relied on their willingness to co-operate.

The 1967 survey of home economics teaching which resulted in a report for the Association compiled by Vincent Hutchinson had as one of its recommendations an end to the practice of using home economics teachers as tea ladies:

> It is accepted in many schools that the domestic science teacher should be responsible for catering for school functions, for visitors and even for the staff. The time has surely come for this policy to change: no other specialist is expected to abandon the content of her lesson to provide a service which only on rare occasions can be educationally justified. The tremendous changes in the interpretation of the subject and in the role of the teacher merits recognition. Provision of refreshments should no longer be regarded as part of the professional duties of a domestic science teacher. (ATDS, 1967, p. 108)

When I began my first teaching practice in the mid seventies I was amazed to see that home economics teachers were expected to turn up after school hours to provide tea for a function which did not even have any connection with their own department. I did not understand why they were prepared to do so. They were surprised to be asked why they accepted this situation, and it was explained to me that it was a normal part of the job and not worth making a fuss about. Clearly the continuance of this practice has for a long time depended on the co-operation of home economics teachers. The complaints made on various occasions have apparently given them an outlet for their feelings rather than provided a way of challenging this aspect of their status in schools to any purpose. They seem to have become trapped in a circle of gender-stereotyped behaviour: expected to behave as subordinates, resenting this but unable to refuse because of their subordinate status.

In a way, too, the use of home economics staff as unofficial caterers at least confirms their 'expert' status, and although they have often resented being seen as little more than cooks, they have also resented the different implication that no particular expertise is involved in the teaching of cookery. One correspondent to *Housecraft* in 1971, for example, complained that primary-school teachers who were not specifically trained in home economics were teaching cookery to pupils in middle schools. She argued that 'such a casual, unstructured approach to the subject will necessitate retraining of the pupils at the upper school stage', and concluded:

> This type of situation does little to improve the status of the subject, for which we have striven for some time. Instead it gives the impression that anyone with a degree of common sense can teach homecraft. (*Housecraft*, July 1971, p. 216)

It is easy to see how home economics teachers, anxious to correct the impression that anyone can do their work, have accepted pressure of the opposing kind which at least implied that they knew better than anyone else how to make the tea.

The fate of marginalisation has been shared in some ways by men teaching the masculine craft subjects woodwork, metalwork and latterly craft, design and technology. Because of their associations with manual trades these have been seen as the province of less academic and predominantly working-class boys. The same arguments about middle-class prejudice against practical subjects have been advanced, with some justification. In a review of the history of design and technology in the school curriculum, Dodd (1978) argued that the desire for higher status had been a constant theme for teachers, and that issues of status and respectability lay concealed in the discussion about titles for heavy craft subjects. (The Design and Technology Working Group referred to this obliquely in its interim report, explaining the decision to use the phrase 'design and technology' and omit any reference to craft.) In terms of working conditions and promotion prospects, women teaching home economics may not have fared particularly worse than men teaching CDT, with the exception that they were less likely to head joint practical-subjects departments. In other ways which are harder to quantify the isolation of home economics teachers within the profession has had more serious effects.

The teaching profession is not a unified whole. In comparing the treatment of one group of specialist teachers with others, it would be misleading to suggest that there is a norm. There is considerable evidence that women teachers in general have worse promotion prospects than men, as well as lower status. The way in which home economics teachers are seen by their colleagues must also depend partly on gender; being seen as apart from or excluded by male colleagues has one meaning, while separation from and exclusion by other women must have another.

Men approve of home economics more than women do, as teachers told me in the conversations I described in the first chapter. This hardly means that men place a high value on it, or view colleagues teaching home economics with exactly the same respect as other teachers. It suggests more that they have been able to approve of the aims of home economics teaching, without the concern for its implications which many women feel. Many women teachers, but few men, have had to study some form of home economics themselves. Its subject area has always taken in the practical detail of women's, rather than men's, domestic lives. It is impossible for women and men to share the same view of it, and hard for some women to feel in sympathy with it.

In school, however unwillingly, women teaching home economics have represented a version of femininity at odds with the reality of life for women who have chosen to teach other subjects. The lack of support from other women of which teachers complained has been part of their experience within the teaching profession, not simply a recent development since feminist criticism of home economics resurfaced. As products of a specific history, home economics teachers can be pictured as on the margins of a wider profession. As agents of a particular ideology, it may be more to the point to see them as inhabiting different territory altogether from other women teachers whose images and educational aims cannot easily coexist with their own.

5

Gateways to Understanding: Home Science and Technology

The great traditional metaphors for education, of doors, light, and keys, can be composed together to form a whole. Going through a gateway from a narrow place into an open space, from darkness and confinement towards light and understanding, expresses in physical terms the student's journey of the mind. Years ago, walking around the city of Oxford for the first time, I looked at the walls and gates of the men's colleges which were then closed to women and remembered Hardy's *Jude the Obscure*. Thomas Hardy wrote about class exclusion but could imagine educated women only as unnatural, lacking femininity and, worse, humanity. He described Jude's exclusion from knowledge as engendering not only anger but a bitter sense of inferiority, but could not see the consequences for women of being even more firmly shut out.

Girls have been given their own separate gateways to learning, as a substitute form of education and a distraction from the fact of the barriers across other entrances. This chapter is about the offering made to girls of a study of home and family as their means to scientific understanding and technical knowledge, and the offering of a limited study of science as their means to a better performance within their homes. Girls have been told that a domestic version of science, and an economics rooted in the home, have a special relevance for them besides being the ones in which they are naturally most interested. It has been pointed out that the laws of science operate within the home as well as outside it; why then should women not learn just a useful selection of scientific laws they can apply or, conversely, study the world from their kitchens?

The invention of domestic science in the late nineteenth century coincided with an uprising of middle-class women seeking access to education. These events, of course, were connected. There was hostility and opposition to the movements for improved secondary education for girls and higher education for women, particularly to the extension of mathematical and scientific education to girls (Dyhouse, 1981). Girls studying science and mathematics beyond the most elementary levels were ridiculed at best, and threatened with the loss of their fertility at worst – neither their brains nor their ovaries were supposed to have been designed to cope with such intellectual labour.

Domestic science was a subject which suited this climate of opinion, deflecting the demand for access to scientific education while still affirming the home as a woman's place. It is tempting to see a conspiracy, but the inherent problems of definition, teacher training and curriculum organisation which led to its failure to become an established mainstream subject also meant that there was uncertain support for it from the start. Writing of the early years of the twentieth century, Catherine Manthorpe noted that there was little evidence of a coherent movement for domestic science teaching in secondary schools despite the interest in it (1986, p. 199).

Bringing science into cookery and household management was not a new idea, but there were few systematic attempts at it until the mid nineteenth century. Influenced by recent discoveries and inventions, with scientific and technical knowledge assuming greater importance in industrialised Britain, it then became something of a minor fashion. In 1857 the century's most prolific author of domestic manuals, Robert Kemp Philp, published *The Housewife's Reason Why*, one of a series of books aiming to make scientific information accessible to the lay reader; it claimed to afford the housewife scientific explanations 'for the various duties she has to perform'. A small proportion of the cookery books appearing in print – including, most famously, Isabella Beeton's *Household Management* (1861) – started to provide information about human nutrition and the composition of foods, based often on Liebig's theories. Their information could only be as accurate as the incomplete and erratic state of knowledge of the time, but accuracy was not always the ᵗⁿᵗ. In *The Gentlewoman* (anonymous, 1864) a superficial impression ⱽanced knowledge clearly took precedence over any other reason ᵗinclusion of scientific jargon. The 'Gentlewoman' quizzes her

soup be made?
be put in a chemically clean saucepan, in cold water, as

> nearly air tight as possible, and simmered at a temperature of 205 to 210 deg.
> If the meat is suffered to boil at 212 deg. all the volatile goodness escapes,
> and the soup is often rendered both empyreumatic and ammoniacal.

Such intrusions of pseudo-science sometimes reflected badly on women's
traditional skills and understanding, and were occasionally resisted. The
story of the 'Norwegian Porridge Feud' is a particularly illuminating example. When Peter Asbjornsen published his book *Fornuftig Madstel*
[Sensible Cookery] in 1864, claiming that 'popular diet and methods of
cooking must be changed to accord with the principles of natural science,
and that women must learn everything anew' (Riddervold and Ropeid,
1989, p. 45), there was an angry reaction from Norwegian women.

The feud centred on a traditional method of cooking porridge, which
Asbjornsen attacked as foolish because the uncooked flour stirred in at
the end of the process could not be digested. Asbjornsen was wrong in
fact, not the Norwegian housewives. His book was based on another by
the German author of a chemical cookery book, Dr Klencke, who had
also written about education arguing that women should be trained for
their work but that only domestic science was relevant for them. Asbjornsen's specific attack on what he characterised as women's ignorance
and superstitious folly was resisted at the time but the general point that
women needed to heed the advice of men educated in science, and needed some relevant scientific education of their own, was taken up in other
quarters.

In Britain the compulsory domestic economy syllabus which girls
in elementary schools were obliged to follow from 1878 onwards included lessons on human physiology and the composition and nutritive value
of food. These effectively substituted for lessons in physical geography,
animal physiology, botany and mathematics, which were taken largely
by boys. As Mary Waring records in her account of elementary-school
science teaching during this period, since girls were not studying other
sciences the teaching of scientific principles within domestic econom[y]
became a matter of concern to the Education Department and to the [In]-
spectors of the School Boards. An Inspector for the London Boa[rd]
example, proposed in 1883 that domestic economy should be[come]
entirely theoretical rather than practical subject, concentratin[g on the]
science of domestic economy, with cookery and laundryw[ork taught]
separately (Waring, 1985, p. 131).

The London Board appointed some peripatetic lad[y]

cluded Mrs Wigley) to teach science to girls in its elementary schools for a few years in the 1890s. The lecturers were supposed to concentrate their teaching on topics relevant to domestic economy, and generally did so, although in one case the Board stepped in to ensure that a scheme of work not based on domestic economy was revised (Waring, 1985, p. 133). From 1897 the system of providing special 'science' lectures for girls was scrapped; instead 'Domestic Science – the Science of Domestic Economy and Hygiene' became an alternative to domestic economy. Waring records:

> In the new course, the Code warned, instruction should be 'entirely ex- perimental, the experiments so far as possible being carried out by the scholars themselves, and arranged with the object of solving a definite pro- blem. Measurement and exact work should be encouraged.' (p. 136)

The sharp gender differentiation apparent in elementary education did not appear so obviously in the secondary schools attended by middle- class girls, where many headmistresses were trying to achieve, as nearly as possible, equal access to the curriculum for their own pupils as for boys in similar schools. Women science teachers, and to some extent domestic subjects teachers themselves, were unhappy about proposals to introduce domestic science and were partly successful in preventing it from supplanting other subjects.

The hero of the domestic science movement in this country was Ar- thur Smithells, Professor of Chemistry at the University of Leeds, whom Catherine Manthorpe describes as 'a leading and influential exponent' (1986, p. 197). Smithells thought that both the traditional version of science teaching, and domestic economy itself, needed reforming. Domestic economy needed a 'solid, scientific foundation'; science itself needed to be made more relevant to the requirements of the ordinary girl.

Smithells was not the only chemistry professor to take an interest in domestic economy and domestic science. William Jackson Pope, author of a series of school readers in domestic economy published in the 1890s, later became Professor of Chemistry at the University of Cam- bridge. Other chemists and physiologists, such as Thomas Cartwright and Henry Major, also compiled or wrote domestic science textbooks for girls. In the preface to *Domestic science* (1900) Cartwright pleaded for girls to be given the same chance as boys to acquire scientific understanding through experimental work, though naturally in a separate context:

> The author entreats the teacher who uses these books to insist on the girls
> working all the experiments with their own hands. His experience with girls
> has taught him that they soon become adepts at manipulation, and that they
> are not one whit behind boys in their power of grasping the truths that the
> experiments are intended to make manifest. Hence he advises ... that the sim-
> ple experiments described should be performed by every girl, who will cer-
> tainly more firmly grasp the fundamentals of Domestic Economy by
> practically proving with her own hands their reality.

There were benefits for male scientists in supporting a separate science
for women, which would avert the prospect of female competition. This
argument has also been advanced to explain the support for domestic
science in America which led to a much more flourishing home
economics movement there. Ellen Swallow Richards, who founded the
movement in America virtually single-handed, had graduated in
chemistry in the face of much discrimination but could not find work.
According to Ehrenreich and English, male scientists closed ranks against
her:

> She could assist the male scientists, befriend them, sew for them, but she
> could not *be one of them*.
> Barred from chemistry, Richards turned her formidable energies toward
> the creation of a new science in which she *would* have a place on an equal
> footing with men. (1979, p. 138)

Ellen Richards's new science was derided by the scientific community at
first, but eventually won some male support. As a movement to preserve
the home and encourage women's interest in housework, it was seen to
have the merit of standing apart from and even opposing the feminist
movement. Ehrenreich and English describe the final outcome of
Richards's career, 'to be honored for founding the science of homemak-
ing', as not so much a triumph as a concession (p. 136).

Women in Britain who were inspired by Ellen Richards's example,
such as Alice Ravenhill, Catherine Schiff and Wenona Hoskyns-
Abrahall, had less ultimate success, perhaps because there were already
a number of women scientists able to argue for girls' access to a
straightforward science education. An interestingly ambivalent case was
that of Marion Bidder, a Cambridge science lecturer who contributed
several chapters to a manual for teachers in training, *Domestic Economy*

in Theory and Practice (1901, reprinted 1911), but argued in 1915 that science and domestic crafts should be kept separate. 'Elementary practical physics and chemistry work should lead to the appreciation of scientific method and scientific accuracy', Bidder maintained (quoted in Manthorpe, 1986 p. 204), while domestic work should be taught as a craft rather than ranked as science.

The ATDS, representing domestic subjects teachers who had not been trained to teach science, had its own proposals on linking science with housecraft which would safeguard their members' jobs. The 'Suggestions' of the Association's special committee set up to consider housecraft teaching in secondary schools were that 'a course of housecraft should form an essential part of a woman's education, and that all girls in Secondary Schools should be given the opportunity of taking such a course' (ATDS, 1911, p. 1). In the ATDS scheme of things girls would take elementary science for the first three years and should be instructed in housecraft for a minimum of two consecutive hours per week, not including needlework, for their last two years in school. The housecraft and science mistresses would correlate their work as far as practicable, so that in physics lessons girls could study heat transference in a way which could be applied to cooking methods, while in chemistry they would learn about air in connection with house ventilation, water in connection with washing, and about a few basic chemicals used in the home.

It is easy to see the benefits such a scheme would bring to the status of domestic subjects and their teachers, and to their acceptability in secondary schools. As long as there was no other form of science education available to girls, it could be argued that domestic science teaching was better than nothing: according to Sara Delamont, 'science could be hidden behind domestic labels' (1978, p. 144). When the proposal was to curtail or circumscribe the science teaching already available, the associations of science mistresses were determined to resist. Correlating physics and chemistry teaching with girls' forthcoming lessons on cookery, laundrywork and home management was hardly going to enhance their status.

Where a separate domestic science was concerned they were understandably afraid, as Manthorpe argues, that it would 'eclipse the progress they had made in developing science studies at school and in sending girls to university to read science' (1986, p. 202). By invading the home, science would 'cut off the valuable privileges that had been won by the pioneers of women's education', in the words of one contemporary writer (Christina Bremner, quoted in Manthorpe, 1986, p. 202).

After the debate documented by Manthorpe ended, there was no doubt that the would-be science of the home had been defeated in its original ambitions by a combination of principled opposition from women science teachers and feminists and official scepticism. The Department and Boards of Education wanted both domestic subjects and science to be taught efficiently, above all, and doubted that domestic science was the answer.

Domestic science lived on, and still lives on, in name and in the margins of the secondary-school curriculum for girls. Without ever having rooted itself in this country as a serious scientific alternative it succeeded, at the expense of generations of girls, in establishing the idea that ordinary science was too masculine for them.

The attempt to provide girls with a scientific education of their own had as its most significant and long-lasting achievement the exclusion of most of them from any higher-level study of physics and chemistry. In addition to the other factors which have recently been studied to explain girls' avoidance of science – its 'masculine' face, the treatment of girls in lessons, biased textbooks and a scarcity of role models for girls – there has been an explicit and deliberate process of differentiation within the curriculum. As Manthorpe argued (1985), this history of differentiation, based on the invention of domestic science as more suitable for them, has kept girls out of mainstream science. It has kept science, in turn, removed from everyday life and preserved its image as masculine and hard.

The idea that subjects like child development, home and family or community care form 'natural' choices for girls (Grafton et al., 1983, p. 153) has been reinforced by their position as alternatives to traditionally masculine subjects when pupils have to make choices for their final years of schooling. One girl in a child development lesson told me she had not really wanted to take it: 'I wanted textiles, I wanted ... but with my other options I couldn't have textiles. I had to choose chemistry, child development or ... one other one ...' When I asked why she had chosen child development rather than chemistry, she simply laughed. She could not believe the question was serious.

There has been no repeat of the early struggle over domestic science, but the attitude that there is something ridiculous about girls studying ordinary science has occasionally resurfaced to provide some justification for the idea of a domestic science. Newsom, for example, in arguing for more gender differentiation in secondary and higher education, described the typical grammar school girl sarcastically as 'far too busy doing her homework and trying to discover the difference between a common and amorphous phosphorus to get down to such a sordid subject as Boeuf Bourguignon or a Creme Caramel' (1948, p. 112). The ATDS was not too squeamish to adopt similar arguments from time to time about the need for girls' education to be made relevant (ATDS, 1961).

Besides the 'relevance' argument, the Association continued to lay stress on the scientific element in domestic subjects, especially at A level and beyond, in the hope that this would give qualifications in domestic science greater credibility and respect. The Association's pamphlet on the value of A levels, published in 1975, summarised the science areas covered by the examinations as:

> Science of food and nutrition. Science of textiles in relation to manufacture, use and care. Science of cleaning materials. Basic scientific principles as applied to housing, furnishing and equipment.

This revealed, according to the Association, that the A level home economics course was academic as well as practical, requiring 'a sound basic knowledge of the physical and biological sciences'. The combination of practical and academic study in this horrible hybrid meant that A level pupils could be asked, for example, to explain the chemical actions of different detergents and soap powders or compare types of washing machine and then recommend suitable equipment for a family of four.

Beyond the often-repeated suggestion that home economics should link up with science, the idea that it could even replace other science courses lingered on or was occasionally revived, until quite recently. In her preface to *Modern Household Science*, a standard textbook for domestic science O level and A level in use throughout the 1970s and into the 1980s, Eva Ling expressed the hope that the book would 'also be found useful as a basis for an Applied Science course for girls in upper forms of secondary schools' (Ling, 1981).

In another example, a case-study of a TVEI course devised by a home economics teacher with the title 'Science in the Home' showed that for some pupils the course held out the promise of an easier, alternative route to a science O level (Evans and Davies, 1988). As the examination board in the end refused to accredit it, their hopes were frustrated. The teacher's own motivation for establishing the course, according to Evans and Davies, was 'to elevate the status of Home Economics teaching by injecting into it a component (science) which she felt or hoped would give it greater *academic* respectability' (p. 42).

Aiming at academic respectability, home economics has continually used science as a cosmetic to deck out its public face. The aims have been as narrow as the content: end-stopped, rather than really seeking to enquire. With the introduction of GCSE, requiring pupils to conduct their own investigations, home economics has once again been presented as a kind of experimental science. Yet although textbooks use the language of science – experiment, control, method – just as domestic economy books did in the last century, and glass dishes from the laboratory may replace kitchen utensils, they have no serious role in guiding pupils towards scientific discovery. Nothing is open-ended; only a few set questions may be asked.

A number of recent textbooks have been designed around tasks which are described as experiments. In one example, *Food Investigations*, intended for pupils in the lower years of secondary school but also to supplement GCSE courses, the author gives instructions for an investigation of carrot cells which calls on pupils to compare raw carrot rings with boiled and grilled carrot rings (Wynn, 1986, p. 26). The purpose of this is not to find out about plant cells but to explain why raw carrots should be boiled rather than grilled.

In another chapter pupils are told how to conduct a controlled experiment in making cakes; they can then deduce that some cake-making methods are to be preferred to others. At the end of the 'cakes experiment' they are instructed to write up their conclusions 'explaining what to do and what not to do when making cakes' (p. 49). The period of discovery has ended; the pupil has tried more or less flour, sugar and heat and arrived at a correct assessment of the right recipe and method. Clearly this road of scientific experiment and discovery is not going to take pupils very far. The end result is hardly different from what would be achieved if they were simply given one recipe and method which they were told to follow, only the process is more cumbersome.

Science invades home economics as a controlling device, insisting on accurate weights and measures as if there were no other ways to cook, trying to 'evaluate' the cries of a baby as a way of comparing the value of a sling and a pram. It also operates as a cloak, covering up the fact that in all-girl classes women teachers are still supervising girls who are washing and ironing tablecloths and teatowels, or comparing ways of cleaning up the kitchens which will one day be theirs.

An assignment in a Nuffield Home Economics textbook asks pupils to spread a mixture of oil and vacuum dust on to a variety of surfaces for an area of about 15 cm × 15 cm, then to clean them with a selection of different products and tabulate the results under the headings 'surface, cleaning agent, number of wipes, length of time, amount of physical energy, observation of results' (Nuffield Home Economics 1985a, p. 110). The format is taken from science, although the pupil is not about to learn any. The teacher's notes advise that 'Pupils should ... draw conclusions about which cleaning substances and methods are most satisfactory for which surfaces' (1985b, p. 148), although they could have drawn similar conclusions from reading the product labels. It is always possible that pupils might feel the hands-on experience of this assignment needs no justification: one of the 'main ideas' behind it, described in the teachers' notes, is that 'Some people find some cleaning tasks very satisfying to carry out' (1985b, p. 147).

Comparison tests of this kind appear to have become very popular, fitting the fashionable frameworks of consumerism, product marketing and 'open-ended' investigation. Girls in one lesson I observed were weighing, counting and tasting sweets from different packets in one such test, tabulating their findings under headings such as 'length of chew'. The immediate purpose was to determine value for money, and nearly all the methods of comparison were based on measurements. There was no scope for asking what value for money meant in this context, although pupils had produced their own posters in another lesson advising people to cut down on sugar. Eating sweets as a sanctioned part of the lesson appealed to most of the pupils. A few girls decided to follow up their work by finding out what was in the sweets, which took them as far as looking up the full descriptions of the ingredients listed as 'E numbers'. Having marvelled at the polysyllabic names, there was nowhere else for them to go with that side of their investigation.

In cookery, the scientific approach serves to stress the utilitarian at the

expense of the aesthetic, as Mennell observed about earlier courses
(1985, p. 231). In child development courses, too, it can be misplaced
when it sends pupils out seeking to monitor the infants' emotional
satisfaction in support of dubious hypotheses.

Hilary Rose has argued that 'the scientisation of domestic work has
actually harmed practice' (1986, p. 71). Particularly where caring for
others is concerned, women already have a body of experiential
knowledge and ways of transmitting it. Rather than adopting a male
model of science, trying to shape women's behaviour in accordance with
an 'increasing scientisation of caring' which can actually erode their confidence, in Rose's view traditional male-defined science should be
challenged and women's existing 'ways of knowing' should be re-
evaluated.

Home economics has been largely untouched by the inconclusive
feminist debate about science as male, to which Rose was contributing.
In its borrowed scientific clothes it is always obliged to follow rather
than to lead. Attempting to prove that it is an intellectually rigorous subject, home economics uses the most traditional model of science without
daring to challenge it or question whether it is always appropriate. Yet
at the same time it is so compromised by its other aims and its inherent
value system that it can never concentrate for long on the task of achieving intellectual rigour. It has so much to measure at once, so many
variables which are not amenable to control.

'Compare the value of a home-made whisked sponge flan case with
an equivalent bought case to a working parent with two young children',
pupils attempting one O level examination in food and nutrition were
asked (University of London, 1986). Having learned something of the
science of nutrition, they are expected to know how to apply it taking
other factors into account, almost as if they were facing a problem in
applied mathematics. One GCSE textbook proposed an investigation
which would control the variable consumer:

> Mrs Jones has identical twin sons aged twenty-one. John works as a computer
> operator. James is a roofing contractor. Both her sons live at home. What
> factors should Mrs Jones consider when planning for her sons?
> Suggest a menu for an evening meal. (Barker, Kimmings and Phillips, 1989,
> p. 96)

The questions which have been excluded still overshadow the question which is asked, in spite of the careful construction of the problem.

Some home economics teachers had hoped to see their subject official-ly linked with science rather than technology once details of the national curriculum became known. Their reasons were often pragmatic: they ex-pected to be able to work more easily with science teachers than with CDT staff. It appears strange that the logical link with technology was denied for so long, while the more tenuous link with science was so often cherished. The reasons must surely be that previously science could offer status, although technology could not, and that the most gendered subjects in the curriculum were forced apart by their identities as feminine and masculine, unable to accept that they had much in common.

When the foundation subject of design and technology, as proposed for the national curriculum, appeared as their means of rescue from obli-vion, home economics teachers at once began the task of re-creating their subject in a new technological mould. NATHE initially welcomed the interim report of the Design and Technology Working Group, although some critics thought home economics had simply been thrown a few compensatory crumbs to make up for its exclusion from the list of sub-jects which were to form the national curriculum. The implications for home economics as a sub-section of design and technology are at the same time encouraging and disturbing. The subject itself stands to gain, but its teachers – almost all women – look set to lose.

The idea that home economics and its craft skills belong in a separate sphere has finally gone, with their logical inclusion as components of design and technology. The Design and Technology Working Group's recommendations offer an escape from past absurdities, and particularly from the tedious insistence within GCSE courses that any study of food or textiles had to be linked to home and family. Although there is still a danger that the implementation of this aspect of the national cur-riculum will lead to more girls doing more cooking and sewing, the em-phasis on design, as I argued earlier, at last gives pupils the possibility of working with food in ways seldom allowed before.

The inclusion of the food and textiles branches of home economics was influenced by a perceived need to make design and technology more 'girl-friendly', at least as much as by NATHE and their supporters. The Working Group had been asked 'to consider ... the expectations and at-titudes of girls to design and technology' (DES and Welsh Office, 1989,

p. 6) and the inclusion of home economics in the list of contributory subject areas was clearly in part a response to this directive.

The Working Group recognised existing gender differentiation as a
problem to be overcome, and warned that it should not be allowed to
continue:

> It will not be possible for pupils to satisfy the requirements of our attainment
> targets and programmes of study by working in a narrow vein of activities,
> e.g. boys working on mechanical and constructional tasks while girls concen-
> trate on catering and textile-related activities. (p. 6)

Beyond recognising the problem and warning teachers, in the space of
one column out of a hundred-page report, the Working Group had little
to say about how the existing almost total division along gender lines
between CDT and home economics could be overcome. It minimised
the need for additional resources, even in the girls' schools which currently lacked any provision for teaching design and technology.

For home economics teachers, the integration of their subject with
CDT presents new status problems. According to the EOC, in 1985 100
per cent of the secondary-school teachers in England qualified in home
economics were women, as were 99 per cent of those qualified in
needlework. For craft-based CDT, 97 per cent of qualified teachers were
men as were 97 per cent qualified in engineering and 91 per cent in
design-based CDT (EOC, 1987). In such traditionally masculine areas,
too, male teachers have been described as likely to hold somewhat 'traditional' views (Grant, 1983; Spear, 1985). With home economics
designated as a minor partner in a consortium of subjects headed by
CDT and information technology, a situation foreshadowed by the wording and emphasis of the proposals for design and technology, many
women teachers are likely to find themselves effectively junior partners
too. It is only too easy to predict who will head the new departments.
In addition to the existing difficulties women in the teaching profession
face in gaining promotion, already likely to be made worse by other pro-
visions of the 1988 Act, home economics teachers have gained credibility at a cost to their autonomy which will inevitably prejudice their future
careers.

The new vision of home economics as a branch of design and
technology also has little room for the areas which are not geared
towards an end product. Stuffed cats, time plans, recipe sheets and nutri-

tion or kitchen layout databases will stay, but exploring issues, discussing feelings, understanding about childbirth or infants when there is nothing in particular to design and make, have no place in an educational programme geared to market forces and business sense.

The influence of the market has already been apparent in child development courses. Looking after a child is often approached in terms of what to buy, or what to make. There is little room to challenge the advertising messages which are even brought into the classroom in armfuls – commercially produced leaflets and store catalogues are a normal part of course materials.

Existing textbooks advise pupils that specially designed tableware for young children is available to make mealtimes more interesting: one obvious place for technological development. Examination assignments and papers require pupils to design and make items suitable for a child to practise or develop one particular skill: the assumption that such one-dimensional toys, of a type already advertised and sold, are desirable and useful passes without question. Under the design and technology umbrella similar 'design and make' projects are likely to proliferate, but there is even less likelihood that fundamental questions about their value can be asked.

The progress made in freeing home economics from notions of servitude, and raising the status of the craft skills which it had become almost ashamed to own, has been checked in turn by the demands and constraints of the market. The marketplace as a setting is supposed to bring realism into the classroom, as though pupils can temporarily suspend their knowledge that they are in school and act as if they are surrounded by a set of immediate economic facts. Instead of seeing themselves as housewives or carers, meeting the needs of others for free, pupils are now to be encouraged to analyse the market and cost their services.

The move from feminine to masculine, softness to hardness, home to marketplace, servicing to selling, results in the recommendations of the Working Group in a curious shift of focus from the food on the plate to the plate itself. In one example of a design and technological activity, pupils are imagined to be redesigning a local amenity hall to help develop community spirit (DES and Welsh Office, 1989, pp. 90–92). There is particular scope for home economics here in the suggestions for work on curtains and refreshment facilities, yet the food and drink to be sold scarcely feature in comparison with the number of references to cutlery, crockery, napkins, storage and sales. In the paragraph headed 'Aesthetics' there is no mention of taste whatsoever, and not even a reference to food except incidentally as something requiring packaging. The design and technological activities listed include:

> ... the design of plates, cups and cutlery for texture, colour, shape; the display of goods on the counter, table cloths and paper napkins; advertising materials; food packaging in order to promote the hall and its ethos. (p. 91).

The changing contexts of home economics appear like a series of place settings as it moves to its next place round the table. At first, girls memorised the recipes they were given by their teachers to produce a thrifty but nourishing meal on an amount they could hope, rather than expect, to be allocated from a labouring man's wages. Next, when money was less of an object, they sequenced and dovetailed their tasks so that their husband's or mother-in-law's meal could be served up on the tablecloth they had laundered while the food was cooking, with an arrangement of flowers nearby and meticulous attention to the final appearance of the dish. In the phase of healthy eating and matching appropriate services to individuals, pupils looked up the composition of foods to produce a meal suited to the particular requirements of the diners (two pensioners, little money, no natural teeth). Now they have first to analyse the market to see what the consumer will buy, work out economies of scale, and dish up the result on a plate they have designed themselves, with matching cutlery and an advertising slogan on the accompanying napkin.

As a would-be science and as a technological activity, home economics has taken on an image of grim rationality which excludes creative expression or play. The scientific or technological format is meant to offer pupils an improved, rigorous, relevant education. For the sake of rescuing their subject, home economics teachers have tended to seize on opportunities to measure anything which can be measured, conduct quantitative surveys, produce design briefs, plans and justifications.

The risk that girls will be offered only a limited version of everything implied in a scientific and technological education has only receded, not gone for good. As a side effect of the rhetoric of equal opportunities, the idea of a girl-friendly science or technology has revived for some the belief that girls have a natural interest in studying soap, cosmetics, curtain design or crockery which should be used to involve them in lessons which otherwise would bore them. It follows from this that girls can be portrayed as naturally less interested than boys in opening their eyes 'to see the wonders of the material universe', as Dorothea Beale put it when she argued that girls' training in home arts ought not to be at the expense of an infinitely wider and more exciting science education.

One appalling fact about the oppression women experience is that some have accepted the doctrine that men really are superior beings. For some, this has had a basis in the simple observation that men know more about the world than women do. The gateways many girls go through are still marked out as separate, and they lead neither to equal rewards nor to an equal level of understanding. There has never been a real equivalence – it has never been seriously suggested that boys should learn science, or develop technological skills, through the medium of home economics. Women whose education took the differentiated, domesticated route know that they know and understand less than their male peers, who were given a more valuable education. Their exclusion was deliberate from the beginning, and the lesson that they could not then claim equal knowledge, understanding and status was hardly less so.

6

Boys: From Sea-cooks to Catering Managers

A boy sings on one of my tape-recordings of a home economics lesson. In the transcript I have noted fourteen bursts of song and thirteen outbreaks of whistling, as well as boys talking in funny voices, jokes, laughter and somewhere a rhythm being played on a saucepan or lid. I have no other tape like this one. It records a fourth-year practical GCSE 'Home Economics: Food' lesson in a boys' school, and confirms evidence from other sources about the important difference between boys' and girls' experiences. Boys have fun in home economics.

Frankie, the boy who sang the most, was in danger of having too much fun. At one point in the lesson the teacher rebuked him, although not in a very serious way:

TEACHER: Frankie, when you come to do a practical exam how are you going to learn to keep quiet? I think you should start practising ... You can smile, we like you looking happy, but try, try to control ...
FRANKIE: I'm only happy when I'm singing.
TEACHER: Then I'm afraid we're going to have to make sure you're sad.

The outstanding feature of this encounter is its rarity. Nothing remotely like this happened in any of the lessons I observed – the majority – where girls were present. Frankie's whole class appeared to share his mood. Girls sometimes told me they liked home economics, but no girl provided such evidence of enjoyment. The mood in other classes, as far as I could detect it, was usually serious and sometimes discontented, but never lighthearted. No girls sang. —> I do.

In recent years feminists have begun to write about the differences between raising sons and raising daughters. The pain, the conflicts and the rewards are not and cannot be the same. Sons grow up to acquire the privileges of maleness in a society dominated by men, while daughters have to learn what it is to be oppressed as girls and women. We need to talk more too about the differences, for women, between teaching boys and teaching girls. Much of the discussion so far has taken as its focus boys' harassment of women teachers, or boys' sexism, and how to deal with them. That is only part of the story. The other part, often acknowledged by staff in mixed schools, is that teaching boys is generally easier. Boys are more likely to reward teachers by showing that they are enjoying themselves. Even their deviancy is more likely to be passed off as a joke.

The quality of the relationship between the teacher in the class described above and her pupils must have owed much to her experience and skills, but the friendliness and lack of stress which make it, unhappily, so exceptional also have a lot to do with gender. The boys were quite clearly placed as children, not as almost-adults, in their relationship with the teacher, yet with no apparent resentment on their side. Their behaviour towards her was dependent, though not always compliant. They saw her as an expert but were also prepared to challenge her:

TEACHER: [to pupil putting spaghetti into pan of water] This is nowhere near boiling.
FRANKIE: So it's still boiled it doesn't matter.
TEACHER: Frankie, if it didn't matter it wouldn't say. Frankie, come here. You did boiling water and how to speed it up last term ...

The boy in this exchange was also the one who sang, and was in too good a mood to stop. Frankie could enjoy the lesson but at the same time make clear that its content didn't much matter. A girl of fourteen or fifteen who was so dismissive of criticism or cared so little for detail – let alone one who had to be told how to boil water – would be making a different kind of statement. As I argue later, whether they are conforming or resisting, home economics has to matter more to girls. Boys have less at stake.

Frankie's teacher was acutely aware of sex stereotyping and sexism as issues in home economics, and confronted boys in her classes on many occasions over their expectations of being serviced, their inability to work co-operatively or their reluctance to discuss 'feminine' topics in a serious way. Her work demonstrated how over-optimistic it is to see boys' entry into home economics in increasing numbers as a straightforward equal-opportunities solution, and showed instead the depth and complexity of gender inequality.

The scramble to transform home economics from a girls' to a gender-free subject may obscure the fact that boys have already been studying it for a long while, sometimes even taking separate specialised boys' courses. In general they have concentrated on cookery, which is still the overwhelming case now. It is comparatively rare for boys to opt for child development courses, and almost unheard of in many areas for them to opt voluntarily for needlework, dress or textiles courses – a teacher in one school told me that she had 'never known a boy to take textiles'. This pattern of choice, which appears so strongly throughout British schools, is not universal. Its cultural specificity is shown up by the example of another school I visited where many of the pupils or their families had come originally from Bangladesh. Because of the high level of demand from boys and their parents, the school had arranged extra classes in tailoring. No girls opted for it, but as a vocational course relevant to their immediate employment prospects it was extremely popular with boys.

Cookery, as a professional activity, has traditionally been dominated by men in terms of the most prestigious jobs and the best pay. There have been many instances of men organising to keep women out of the male profession of cookery (for examples see Mennell, 1985; Attar, 1986). Only the domestic, unpaid version has been universally allotted to women. In training and education this has led to a predictable split, with boys going off to colleges to take vocational courses in catering, often leading to the City and Guilds of London Institute qualifications which are required for many jobs, while girls take courses at school which concentrate on cookery for home and family and gain them professionally useless qualifications, if any.

College catering courses have had a distinctly masculine image. It used to be difficult for girls to gain entry to them, and girls were often steered towards the least skilled and least well-paid fields. This was logical since it was consistent with discriminatory employment practices. Courses were linked to apprenticeship schemes which excluded girls, and orientated towards the requirements of large hotels and restaurants which would employ only men as chefs. One standard textbook in use throughout the 1960s and seventies, John Fuller's *Chef's Manual of Kit-*

chen Management (1962), covering the City and Guilds cookery syllabuses amongst others, assumed throughout that chefs and students were male. The few references to women located them mainly as unskilled or semi-skilled workers employed as kitchen hands, or at best as breakfast cooks in hotels, with only minor responsibilities. Its author also acknowledged, as an exception, the existence of the 'high grade working woman cook' (a limiting description which has no male counterpart) in a small establishment serving English fare, who could be a more realistic proposition than an actual chef but could not receive the appellation 'chef' herself.

The division between professional training together with formal apprenticeships for boys, and school lessons serving as informal domestic apprenticeships for girls, led to another split in the content of food and cookery teaching. For boys, the emphasis was placed on the craft skills they needed to compete in the labour market, not on the themes of sound nutrition and thrift which were constantly emphasised to girls. In the annual catering competitions which gave young trainees – almost always male – a chance to show off their skills, the great set pieces were traditionally required to be impressive displays of technical proficiency; they did not have to be particularly edible.

The NACNE and COMA reports (1983 and 1984) advising changes in the average British diet made the divergence between the goals of the separate examining bodies for the two sectors even more apparent. Although – as Brenda Pratt (quoted above) had pointed out – home economics lagged behind health education in turning its attention to nutrition and health, the influence of these reports showed up very quickly in examination syllabuses. Meanwhile a survey of catering courses in the London area in 1985 found that few college catering departments were giving priority to trends towards healthy eating, at a time when this was becoming a dominant feature of home economics courses in schools. In their replies some college departments identified 'present syllabus guidelines ... as a constraint to development of a more health-conscious approach to catering' (Brunner, 1985).

Within schools, too, home economics for boys has had its own separate history. In the early years of domestic economy teaching, boys living in seaport towns were given a special dispensation by the Board of Education to attend cookery classes in the elementary schools (Yoxall, 1913, p. 49). It was otherwise almost unheard of for boys to take domestic subjects, and in the period of payments by results they could not be counted towards the grant if by some chance they were entered for examination along with the girls.

When any consideration was given to cookery lessons for boys it was always within a specific, limited and well-defined context. If they were not prospective sea-cooks, boys wanting to take cookery lessons were probably Boy Scouts. Yoxall, who in 1913 mistakenly thought that 'the question of cookery instruction for boys in general will soon receive careful consideration', wrote that Boy Scouts often asked if they could join classes as they needed to learn to make porridge and soup in order to become Scouts of the first class.

Boy Scouts were still featuring nearly sixty years later, when the Curriculum Development Committee of the ATDS was considering the teaching of domestic science to boys and an issue of *Housecraft* was devoted mainly to various aspects of the topic. The contributors took for granted that courses for boys were generally provided separately, and were different from the usual courses which were for girls. One article on teaching cookery to a Scout patrol concluded that boys were now 'ready and willing to enter the world of home economics' (Forbes and Gillett, 1971), but it was still clear that they were far from ready to enter on equal terms.

From teachers' accounts of their work it emerged that courses for boys could be of three types: vocational in the serious sense of equipping them for paid employment once they left school; purely recreational; or basic, in the form of short 'survival' courses preparing them for looking after themselves in circumstances which were seen as exceptional rather than normal.

As a vocational subject for boys, in some cases cookery was still a route to joining the navy. A teacher in Wales explained that many of the boys who chose cookery in her school were also likely to go to sea, and related their choice to the general employment situation. This allowed her to accept a choice which, as her account showed, she could not have accepted without such conditions:

> We encourage boys to take cookery if they have a genuine interest and wish to make it their career ... this is because they can get training for employment as chefs and waiters at a nearby college's Hotel Catering Department, and in an area of low employment this provides well paid work. (Whitfield, 1971)

Several of the boys I spoke to in mixed schools in 1988 who had chosen home economics – but none of the girls – mentioned wanting to be a chef as their reason for taking it. Some may really have had serious ambitions to become chefs, but their answers also reflected the pressure they were under from teachers, parents and other pupils to provide an acceptable motive, compared with girls who did not have to explain themselves and need give no reason at all.

There was little general agreement in the early 1970s about overcoming what some home economics teachers saw as old-fashioned prejudice against changing sex roles. For several contributors the best method of introducing domestic science for boys was by creating masculine courses and emphasising that this was not 'girls' stuff', as one headmaster discussing how it could be introduced into the curriculum of a boys' school phrased it:

> At all times it is important to avoid the feeling of 'girls' stuff', and probably the safest way to start would be to offer catering as an optional fourth year subject with heavy stress upon the vocational aspect.
>
> The introduction of a catering course would make it necessary to have special accommodation provided. To maintain the important distinction between girls' cookery and catering the room should perhaps be organised and equipped along the lines of hotel and service kitchens, that is, a centre island for cooking, with preparation and washing/cleaning areas around the perimeter of the room. (Brockman, 1971)

The kitchen layout Brockman recommended is of course designed for a staff organised hierarchically, not for individuals expected to do all their own preparation and clearing up as most home economics pupils are. His interest in such an arrangement does draw attention to the limitations of the traditional home economics room, typically divided into a number of self-contained workspaces each shared by a small group or a pair of pupils. The 'important distinction' which Brockman wanted to preserve and emphasise, rather than challenge, was not only a visible distinction or a question of status and identity. It had other implications for teaching and learning styles, since the standard arrangement he shrank from as inappropriately feminine is not planned for larger-scale teamwork, while his suggested layout is not intended for workers of equal status combining their efforts. The two arrangements were designed not only for efficiency in contrasting settings, but to meet the demands of different divisions of labour.

Attitudes towards cooking as a recreational subject for boys have varied according to pupils' ages and abilities. For boys in a school for slow learners, pastry-making could be seen as a therapeutic extension of sand and water play, according to one teacher (Hinsley, 1971). For sixth-formers who could afford to choose additional courses for no very serious reason, cooking could be enjoyed as a hobby.

Two pupils who provided personal accounts of their experience of recreational home economics in the *Housecraft* special issue made the point that boys had to face taunts of homosexuality from their peers if they did choose it:

> ... you will probably have to withstand being called a sissy, bent, queer, etc. but don't give it up ... (Jaques, 1971)

> ... many people consider boys who enjoy cooking rather 'effeminate' and this is such a pity ... it dissuades many from taking it up as a hobby. (Dick, 1971)

The opportunity to cross sex-role boundaries could none the less be attractive and could offer boys easy access to high achievement, or at least a sense of it, since they were only comparing themselves with girls. One pupil described how he chose home economics because he wanted to do something different, and thought it would be a challenge to himself and to the girls in his class. He eventually formed an ambition to become a lecturer in food and nutrition at a home economics college. The conspicuous position this pupil was in seems to have worked to enhance his self-esteem and confidence. As Jenny Shaw (1984) has pointed out, boys in mixed classes tend to see girls as a 'negative reference group' and assume either that girls are performing worse than themselves or that girls' superior performance can be discounted. When girls form the only reference group and a boy taking home economics can consider his mere presence on a course as outstanding, it is understandable that he could easily perceive himself as doing extremely well and ready to aim for the furthest point ahead that he can see.

Most courses designed specifically for boys were of the 'bachelor living' type, aiming to teach them a handful of essential facts and skills for looking after themselves. In the *Housecraft* articles, teachers referred specifically and repeatedly to a need for boys to learn how to look after *themselves*, with no suggestion that they might also have to look after others.

Nutrition education for boys also tended to place them as consumers rather than providers. One teacher even argued that disharmony in the home was created by men's faulty eating habits, because they rejected their wives' attempts to offer them a more varied diet. The answer to this was to teach boys nutrition so that they would be more appreciative of their future wives' efforts. The traditional rationale, given or accepted by boys, for learning to cook the few quick, convenience meals these courses featured was that in a crisis they might need to fend for themselves – when a girlfriend walked out, or a wife was in hospital.

The emphasis in other branches of home economics was again on personal care, described as 'good grooming' or 'valeting', with a minimal amount of attention paid to what used to be called laundrywork – one teacher wrote that she was considering taking her group of sixth-form boys on a visit to a launderette next time the course ran. Wording was important: boys were not to be taught 'housecraft' (then a CSE subject for girls) but could study 'home care and maintenance'. Money management and budgeting, which had a sufficiently masculine appeal, were considered vital ingredients of home economics courses for boys.

One London teacher argued that teaching about hygiene and grooming could enable boys to take advantage of the home-like ambience of the home economics department, a privilege usually enjoyed exclusively by girls:

> Boys ... should be equally welcome to join in the lunch-time freedoms which girls have always had – to pop in to remove a stain, sew on a button, wash and iron a muddied shirt to prevent a 'telling-off' from an overworked mum, or just to offer help in getting something repaired or ready for the next lesson. We know that for the most part they are all excuses to come for a chat. The housecraft room really is the home within the school and girls have tended to regard this as their own – a jealously guarded sanctum. (Myers, 1971)

There have been few signs at any period that girls were going to lose their sanctum to boys, as the numbers on these courses were always small. The ATDS survey of four hundred and twenty-five mixed schools in 1967 found that in nearly half no boys at all were participating in domestic science lessons. The number of boys taking domestic science in the remaining schools was tiny. Sixty of the schools offered single-sex classes for boys, although it was never a compulsory subject for them, as it frequently was for girls. The peak year for boys' participation was the fourth year of secondary school, although only forty-two schools had ten or more fourth-year boys taking domestic science. Far fewer younger boys or older boys were reported to be taking it. Although boys' involvement was restricted to particular school years, in almost all the schools in which boys were offered domestic science fewer than six in any year group were actually taking it (ATDS, 1967).

The survey also reported teachers' views on the subject areas within domestic science which held the most interest for boys. Cookery came first by a wide margin, followed in order by household repairs, household management, family relationships and health education. The most interesting feature of this survey finding is that it is indicative of a quite different curriculum from that usually followed by girls. More than a third of the schools which did offer domestic science to boys reported that they planned courses with their interests in mind. No boys' schools were surveyed, but the author commented that it was fairly obvious that little provision was being made in boys' schools for domestic science teaching.

The era of supposed equal opportunities put an end to the provision of separate courses for boys in mixed schools, although it did not bring about equality between schools. In the late 1980s home economics departments in boys' schools were still unusual. A Kent teacher wrote in 1987 of the hard work needed 'to establish a Home Economics department in a secondary boys school' (*Modus*, 1987) and several London boys' schools were still at the stage of hoping to start their own departments. They faced the problem of a scarcity of resources, shared also by schools which had set up home economics departments. One teacher I spoke to in a boys' school calculated that craft, design and technology had six times the resources of her own department and said it gave the impression of occupying a vast proportion of the school's space, whilst she had one room and was the sole teacher in her subject area.

Boys who do choose home economics seem in general to come from a narrower range of ability groups, and probably also a more unified social class background, than the girls. Examination statistics show not only that relatively few boys choose home economics compared with girls (see the tables in Chapter 2) but also that their examination results are considerably worse. The margin of difference between boys' and girls' performance is significantly greater than the average difference, in girls' favour, for pupils taking GCE or CSE. This pattern of difference, shown in Table 4, appears fairly consistently in tables of examination

Table 4 Comparison of boys' and girls' results in JMB Home Economics (Food) GCE ordinary level examinations[1]

	1984–5 (%)			1985–6 (%)			1986–7 (%)		
	No.	C+	E+	No.	C+	E+	No.	C+	E+
Girls	23,682	39.2	69.6	24,579	66.7	73.0	26,489	40.5	75.8
Boys	2,762	13.6	39.2	3,379	16.3	46.2	4,556	16.6	51.1

Source: Adapted from Joint Matriculation Board Statistics of Examinations, Manchester, 1986, 1987, 1988.

1. Including Joint O level/CSE and Alternative Ordinary examinations.

results, whenever the number of boys concerned is large enough for comparisons to be made.

As so few boys take advanced level home economics, or branches other than food at GCE/CSE level, it is more difficult to draw conclusions about boys' comparative results in these areas, although some A level tables do show boys performing significantly worse. More often the numbers are so small that a high percentage of good grades reflects the success of just a couple of boys. The JMB statistics, for example, show that 100 per cent of the boys who took Home Economics: Child Care ordinary level in 1987 gained a Grade E, though none gained Grade C or above. This refers to the fact that one boy took the examination, and he passed.

The examples in Tables 4 and 5 reveal a wide gap between boys' and girls' achievements, which needs to be explained. Boys taking these examinations were at least twice as likely to fail – and in one case about five times as likely – as girls. Girls' greater familiarity with the content of the course – and even boys' over-confidence, as discussed above – are possible factors, but the most plausible explanation lies in the screening process which lets some pupils into home economics, and keeps others out.

The minority of boys who opt for home economics are likely to be perceived as less academically able ('opting' can of course be a misleading word; the boys from a lower-stream class who were timetabled to do home economics 'as a joke' in the incident described in the last chapter presumably were not given much option at all). In one case-study of

Table 5 Grades achieved by percentages of girls and boys in a sample of O level home economics examinations, June 1983

	A	B	C	D	E	U	Total number
Girls							
AEB	5.0	21.9	37.0	16.6	16.9	2.6	13,812
London	6.7	26.1	34.4	11.0	8.7	13.1	6,661
Boys							
AEB	2.4	9.2	29.0	15.6	31.6	12.1	620
London	1.2	15.1	30.6	14.3	9.7	29.1	258

Source: Adapted from University of London and Associated Examining Board GCE Examination Statistics, 1984.

gender and curriculum choice, the very few boys taking a fourth- and fifth-year 'family and child' course were all from a remedial group and left at Easter without taking the examination (Grafton *et al.*, 1983, p. 158). Clever boys don't choose, or are not allowed to choose, home economics; clever girls are discouraged too, as the ATDS often used to complain, but not nearly to the same extent. Boys' career prospects matter more than girls' do – to parents, schools, and not least to pupils themselves. The low-status subject of home economics is regarded as good enough for a few boys without much expectation of academic achievement, but not for the rest. It is good enough for girls, though, even if they are academically able.

Teachers who perceive this ability gap sometimes explain boys' choice of home economics in terms of their appetites. 'Antony isn't interested in Food [GCSE Home Economics: Food], he's just interested in feeding his face, that's the only reason he comes', a teacher in one mixed school explained. This view of boys' involvement seems to have been shared by many other teachers, and allows for the fact that boys are not as likely as girls to do well or to take the subject seriously. A teacher in a boys' school explained in a *Modus* article in 1987 that her pupils needed short-term goals to work for, as many of them were 'solely motivated by the call of the adolescent stomach'. Such remarks are never made about girls, even those viewed as academically weak.

In the mixed lessons I observed, teachers were generally on the lookout for boys trying to pass their share of tidying or washing up on to the girls in the class, although it still sometimes happened. The greatest difference I noticed between girls and boys was in calling-out behaviour – boys were much more likely to call out to the teacher, and often seemed to think a whistle would fetch her over to them. They were usually seeking the answer to a question the girls did not need to ask, such as what to do with an empty tin, or where to look for ingredients or equipment.

The most marked example of this type of behaviour occurred not in a mixed class, but in a boys' school. My tape-recorder had been stolen (not from school premises) and I had to decide at short notice what to note down about the third-year practical I was about to observe. Within a few minutes the answer became obvious, because the boys' behaviour towards the teacher was so outstandingly different from anything I had seen in other schools. The frequency of the pupils' demands reminded me more of children at home with their mothers than of scenes in other schools.

The impromptu observation schedule I drew up recorded a total of ninety-two requests for the teacher's attention in the space of forty-six minutes, in addition to another twenty-three shouts of 'Miss!' and occasional whistles directed at her. From where I sat I could not observe the whole room, so my total was certainly an underestimate, besides leaving out of the count the first few minutes of the lesson. Boys seeking the teacher's attention often went up to her, physically surrounding her or following her around the room. As there were occasional periods of comparative calm, there were also periods of frantic persistence on the part of pupils, with as many as five boys trying to get her attention at once. There were fifteen boys in the class, and their task was to prepare and eat a snack – sandwiches, or baked beans on toast, with a drink.

A number of studies have shown that boys demand more teacher time and attention than girls (for example Spender, 1982; Stanworth, 1983). In the example above, where there was no question of competition between boys and girls, the physical situation – a class of boys with one woman teacher, in a room which was effectively a kitchen – seemed to intensify this pattern of behaviour. Boys' tendency to monopolise equipment in mixed classes has also been recorded (see, for example, Kelly, 1985). While I noted no particular instances of this in the lessons I saw (and I had not set out to record any), something else struck me: boys were more likely to use machinery unnecessarily. Neil, in the lesson described in the first chapter, used a food processor to slice a single tomato. Girls were not denied access to machines, but did not use them without good reason.

In the past teachers have seized on machines as a way of drawing boys into home economics, along with the opportunity to fix things and fiddle with hardware in general:

> ... Boys have a natural curiosity that stimulates the development of every lesson. Water and waste pipes are trailed to their destinations and they want to know how all equipment works. There is never any shortage of willing hands to mend a sink plug and check loose screws on grill pans or ideas to reorganise work space and assist with furnishing the housecraft flat. (Myers, 1971)

> ... The popularity of needlework for the boys was less predictable [than for cookery], there is no doubt that the electric sewing machines were an attraction ... (Ellwood, 1971)

> Teaching the carrying out of 'handyman' jobs in the home is, I feel, the task of the craft teacher. However, I do find that the boys will voluntarily get a screwdriver to tighten up a loose screw. (Hinsley, 1971)

> Boys will gladly mend the wall can opener, screw on glass oven doors and spend ages discovering why the mixer goes clonk clonk instead of clink clink ... (Gillett, 1971)

More recently computers and industrial machinery have been brought into home economics, to help establish its new identity as a branch of design and technology while also, deliberately or coincidentally, making it more masculine. The greatest change has probably happened within textiles as a school subject. Needlework was once the most feminine subject of all, and as such repelled boys almost without exception. Now that some courses have been redefined and turned into textiles technology, with computer-programmable knitting machines and industrial overlockers taking the place of familiar domestic equipment, they aim to attract the interest of many more boys (though as yet there is little evidence of their success). In a sense the new curricular environment of technology represents a return to craft skills as the essential basis of home economics, with industrial and commercial settings replacing the traditional domestic context.

Courses which focus on the industrial uses of food and textiles technology, rather than seeing food and textiles as linked elements of one overarching subject concerned with home and family life, are more compatible with the aims of the national curriculum than with the criteria for GCSE examinations. (The construction of home economics as technology is discussed more fully in the previous chapter.) Design and technology, as envisaged by the national curriculum working party, will change the whole framework for teaching home economics, and in one very specific sense will make textiles and food courses more masculine. Although pupils' design briefs are supposed to relate to home life and leisure activities as well as to manufacturing and retailing, when the underlying model for their activities has been derived from commerce and industry rather than from the home the stress falls very differently.

Shedding the 'soft' image of home economics so that it can compete with the 'harder' areas of design and technology also conflicts with the use of home economics as an anti-sexism training ground. Teachers who ran 'skills for living' and anti-sexism courses in a small number of boys' schools (described in, for example, Askew and Ross, 1988), far from trying to make home economics masculine, were asking boys to look at and challenge their own assumptions about male and female roles. It was essential to these courses to preserve and use home economics' emphasis on home and family, both as a way of socialising boys into more caring and co-operative forms of behaviour and to make the point that the home was not only, or necessarily, a woman's place.

Some teachers foresaw the danger of converting home economics into a subject with more masculine appeal, at the expense of its potential for changing traditional attitudes. In the 'Home economics and child development' section of *Genderwatch!*, an in-service training pack for teachers produced by the EOC and the School Curriculum Development Committee in 1987, Nicky Wadsworth questioned teachers in boys' schools about the approaches they took:

> Are the male pupils encouraged to develop their capacity for caring, supportive and co-operative behaviour?
>
> Are the male pupils encouraged to empathise, share and show emotion?
>
> Do you emphasise catering rather than life skills? (Wadsworth, 1987, p. 181)

Compared with the efforts which have been made since around 1980 (Kelly, 1985) to encourage more girls into science and technology, the efforts of the small number of teachers and advisers concerned with the role of home economics in boys' education have been almost insignificant. Girls' lack of participation in scientific and technological education at sixteen and beyond was seen to have serious consequences for themselves and for the whole of society, and as a problem demanding a number of approaches. Researchers examined classroom behaviour, teacher attitudes, course materials and careers advice and generally concluded that everything needed to change. There was no parallel development for home economics, in spite of evidence that it was the worst case of gender differentiation in the curriculum.

Boys' lack of participation in home economics was simply not seen as the same order of problem; the textbook and syllabus changes prompted by equal-opportunities legislation and regulations were not supported by a thorough appraisal of classroom practice, and certainly not by high-level expressions of concern. Home economics teachers themselves did complain about this one-sidedness, which one *Modus* editorial (addressed to Kenneth Baker) argued was not only unfair but was also undercutting their own pupil numbers and resources:

> ... Schools should be convincing *boys* and their parents of the value of non-traditional subjects ... Put bluntly, there must be a two-way traffic so that in pursuit of one good cause – girls into science and technology – another good cause – Home Economics – is not vitiated and impoverished.

Even in the field of gender and education, there was little interest in looking at gaps in boys' education until the late 1980s. The first feminist scrutiny of home economics to result from the new wave of feminism dating from the 1970s set out to detect forms of blatant stereotyping and pressures towards domesticity aimed at girls. The question of boys' participation was raised only briefly as an issue of equal opportunities. Wynn (1983), for example, argued that home economics teaching ought to reflect and encourage equal roles in the home for men and women.

Equal opportunities were still the theme of the *Genderwatch!* self-assessment notes for teachers quoted above, but the approach Nicky Wadsworth advocated went beyond making home economics gender-free or offering it on an equal basis to boys and girls. She raised the issue of the nature of boys' participation, asking whether they were taking the same type of course as girls or experiencing the same type of involvement. She suggested, too, that home economics teaching could in some way compensate boys for deficiencies in their education or upbringing.

The basis for her approach was nevertheless still equal opportunities. In presenting sex differentiation in home economics as simply a reversal of the situation of male domination in science and technology, Wadsworth produced a strangely unreal account of the 'problem' of female domination.

Using a model of male domination in mixed classes as described by a number of researchers, Wadsworth asked teachers to consider whether the group leaders in mixed classes were always female, and whether compensatory support was offered to male pupils (1987, p. 181). Referring specifically to 'female dominance within home economics', she asked:

> If the subject is taught only by females, what attempts have you made to encourage male colleagues to collaborate with and support your teaching? Do you use the expertise of male colleagues and therefore encourage positive role models for male and female pupils? (p. 180)

Another question indicated how male support could be engaged: 'Do you encourage male colleagues to come to your lessons and share their culinary expertise?' (p. 184). The list of 'strategies for change' again stressed male teachers as a resource, recommending: 'Male teachers in schools should be encouraged to participate in teaching every aspect of the subject, working alongside qualified female staff' (p. 185).

On the question of adapting courses to encourage boys into home economics, the recommendations were much less clear. Teachers were asked whether they had considered 'introducing any changes to encourage more male pupils to opt for home economics' (p. 186), but as they were also advised not to let boys concentrate on catering or emphasise the narrowly vocational aspects of the subject, the potential nature of such change was unexplained.

It is unlikely that many teachers found it necessary to address the 'problem' of girls' dominance, which appeared to have been deduced by analogy and, to judge from my own observations of lessons where teachers had to prevent boys from getting girls to do their chores, is more mythical than real. The proposal that men, in the form of valuable role models, should contribute their 'expertise' is much more disturbing. I find Wadsworth's concern for their absence entirely misplaced, since in reality male 'expertise' is promoted as visibly in cookery as it is in most other fields, as every schoolboy knows (and often says).

Maleness alone, in the *Genderwatch!* proposals, provides enough of a qualification for male colleagues to help each 'every aspect of the subject', alongside 'qualified' female staff. Yet pupils are not supposed to draw the obvious lesson from this – that men have more authority and expertise than women, as television commercials, cookery programmes and countless other sources have already told them. Instead it is envisaged that they will only receive the message (assumed to be something of a new idea to them) that men, too, can cook, care for children and take an interest in home and family life.

More recently, Geen (1989) has provided an expanded account of the problem of female dominance, and suggested strategies for dealing with it. Again, the visibility of men already dominating 'female' areas was implicitly denied:

> Not only does a male presence help to eradicate the traditional view of the subject as one dominated by women, but it also demonstrates to pupils beyond any shadow of doubt that both sexes are equally able to master [sic] skills in this area of the curriculum. (p. 147)

Geen argued that for the foreseeable future home economists would 'have to maintain the practice of inviting into their departments as many men as possible from outside the educational system', but even when considering the role models such men could provide seemed unaware of the contradiction. In some of the schools Geen surveyed, the policy had already been adopted:

> ... males occupying 'non-traditional' roles (e.g. male spinners, florists, nurses and hairdressers) had addressed pupils; in others chefs, restaurateurs and employees in the food industry participated in pre-vocational initiatives. (p. 147)

It is difficult to see what problem Geen is trying to solve, since there is clear evidence that male employees in the food industry, chefs and restaurateurs already enjoy much greater access to vocational training than their female counterparts. In 1985, for instance, figures from the DES showed that nearly twenty-five thousand male students aged between sixteen and twenty were released by their employers for training in the hotel, catering, miscellaneous service, food, drink and tobacco industries, compared with just over eighteen thousand girls (EOC, 1987).

The view of female dominance as a problem, which I think is misconceived, arises from an attempt to see home economics as a subject exactly like any other except with the power relations changed around. Boys' reluctance to choose it can then be seen as a consequence of stereotyping which can be dealt with by a shift of emphasis towards boys and men. An alternative feminist view in the 1980s took a harder look at boys' conditioning, and offered courses in home economics as a means almost of civilising pupils who were pictured as unable to work co-operatively or express their gentler emotions without what amounted to remedial help.

One aim of the small number of anti-sexism courses introduced into a few London boys' schools in the 1980s, according to Sue Askew and Carol Ross, was to

> ... provide equal curriculum opportunities (including childcare studies and domestic crafts) to help boys to learn to take domestic responsibility and not to regard this as a woman's realm. (1988, p. 75)

The authors were aware that providing a basic level of information and skill would not be enough to guarantee future domestic equality:

> Learning to cook, or learning about children, does not necessarily change boys' stereotyped notions about roles in the home. We have often heard comments such as: 'It's useful for when my wife goes into hospital' or 'It's a good idea because I might be on my own for a while before I get married'. (p. 75)

They advocated challenging boys directly or indirectly about their attitudes, looking at stereotyping itself and at boys' concepts of masculinity. Rather than simply teaching skills and imparting knowledge, home economics lessons in some schools were used to develop the social skills which boys were seen to lack:

> For example, boys worked together in a small group making a meal and then eating it (often with a guest), as an opportunity to develop their ability to work collaboratively as well as develop a sense of responsibility for another person's well-being. The assessment built into the work allowed the boys to reflect, not on how good their finished food was but on how well they have worked together.

The courses described by Askew and Ross were mainly compulsory courses for boys in the early years of secondary education at single-sex schools. It was the aggressive and often misogynist ethos of boys' schools, as much as anything, which set the scene for the type of com-

pensatory education they offered. In common with the *Genderwatch!*
recommendations, they stressed the necessity for boys to learn about
parental responsibilities and the needs of young children, but as a way
of understanding themselves too. The authors acknowledged that there
were limits to what could be achieved by such courses on their own,
when boys' schools were socialising pupils in a different direction in so
many other ways.

The concept of boys' inadequacy as a problem for home economics
to solve is as unconvincing to me as the problem of female dominance.
There is enough available evidence that boys, and men, are able to work
co-operatively when they wish to (leaving aside some more dubious
theories about male bonding). Learning how to behave as a member of
a football team arguably involves at least as much skill in co-operation
as learning to make tea and toast.

The argument for compensatory lessons in boys' schools rests on the
belief that boys receive an unbalanced education, and an inadequate
social training, in single-sex schools which provide them with an unplea-
sant and sexist environment. One-off courses offer some redress, but the
root problem of single-sex schools for boys remains. By definition, they
provide a single-sex education, historically designed to be not only different from girls' education, but better. There is a fundamental contradiction between the institution of a boys' school and a course in
anti-sexism. Courses which deal in essence with the women and girls
who are physically absent, setting out to teach classes exclusively of boys
about parenthood, childbirth and childcare, may create as many problems as they set out to solve. In a historical context there is nothing
new or necessarily radical about all-male classes studying women and
women's lives, and announcing their objective expertise.

Strategies for dealing with female dominance or with boys' inadequacy
start from the same assumption: that boys have a problem with home
economics, which it could be restructured to solve. My observation of
boys' lessons led me to the opposite conclusion. Boys do not appear to
have problems with home economics (other than the one they share
with girls of trying to understand what the subject is now supposed to
be about). They have more freedom to enjoy it than girls do, and are
more likely to reap praise from their teachers. If they do not choose
home economics options (and few academically able boys do), their decisions are not the unthinking result of stereotyping but have an entirely

rational basis. They judge home economics as not particularly valuable for them in the future, compared with other subjects – and in general they judge correctly.

Accounts of home economics lessons as a form of anti-sexist evangelism and accounts of traditional lessons a generation earlier are united by one theme: it is wonderfully rewarding to teach boys. I heard boys praised for taking an interest in the facts of childbirth, for owning their own pairs of rubber gloves, for saying that they wash up at home. Most of all, it seems that boys endear themselves to their teachers because they are having so much fun.

Reading the past thoughts of home economics teachers on teaching boys, easily the most striking feature, absent from descriptions of teaching home economics to girls, is the enjoyment which both teachers and pupils express. In all the literature I have surveyed, girls may be represented as 'bustling', 'pottering', 'competent', 'interested', 'enthusiastic', 'responsible' and so on, but there is never much doubt that they are rehearsing for the serious business of adult life. They are not shown as simply having fun, like the 'lads' who decorated a pie 'not with pastry leaves but "Chelsea for the Cup" ' (Gillett, 1971, p. 197). Nor are girls shown as satisfying their own appetites, like the former pupil explaining that he opted for home economics because of his 'gluttony'.

Boys' greater interest and enjoyment have been noted time and again, although without any attempt to explain them unless in terms of boys' relative childishness. The ATDS curriculum committee which considered the teaching of home economics to boys wrote in a *Housecraft* article: '... those who have taught this subject to boys find that they show a keen interest, often more than girls'. Contributors to the same issue (on teaching boys) praised their 'natural curiosity' and 'genuine interest', wrote of 'fun', 'sheer pleasure', of tasks that boys 'gladly' do; one teacher noted that boys bring 'real enthusiasm', while another commented: 'Boys show more enthusiasm than girls and give down-to-earth reasons for wanting to cook' (p. 191).

Boys came in for gushing praise and were clearly expected to know and care a lot less than they actually did, so that their achievements were disproportionately admired:

They buy their own fabric and since they do not have much experience, very often the fabric is difficult to handle, uneven stripes and checks, slippery

satin, fine lawns, but they have a definite sense of colour and seldom do their
ties clash with their shirts ... With painful persistence they match almost all
the checks and produce fine French or run and fell seams ... (Myers, 1971)

A teacher in a further-education college, writing that the sheer pleasure
boys got from making meat patties, apple pies and doughnuts had to be
seen to be believed, found that ... 'the nicest thing about teaching boys
is their sense of humour, they never burst into tears when things go
wrong or get in a flap' (Gillett, 1971). She asked rhetorically: 'Who but
a boy would decorate a pie not with pastry leaves but 'Chelsea for the
Cup' and plan real turtle soup and stuffed grouse for his next lesson ...'

Who indeed. It is more pertinent to ask when girls were ever praised
for their curiosity or wild and clumsy enthusiasm. Yet the paeons of
praise for the keenness of boys still rang late into the 1980s. One article
about setting up a home economics course in a boys' school described
the need to bring all the enthusiasm into order (Bell, 1987): it is still
boys' unthinking enjoyment, rather than their lack of interest, which
creates problems for teachers.

The question is not whether boys really are so wonderful; as I argued
before, in some ways teaching boys may offer greater rewards. A more
important question is whether the praise they collect is at the expense
of girls, whose achievements in home economics (let alone their posses-
sion of aprons and rubber gloves, endearing persistence at hemming or
failures to match every last check) are not so unequivocally admired.

Teachers undoubtedly have lower expectations of boys in home
economics, as expressed in the *Genderwatch!* suggestion that they be offered compensatory teaching. There is also evidence that in other subjects boys and girls are praised for different achievements and behaviour,
with boys assumed to have more natural curiosity and enthusiasm (see,
for example, Walkerdine *et al.*, 1989). Yet the observable difference between boys and girls in home economics needs more of an explanation.
Boys' enthusiasm, despite the attention it gets, does not really need to
be explained, but as I argue in the last chapter of this book, there are
many reasons why girls should have to stifle theirs.

The effect of gender on home economics is an infinitely more subtle
matter than the question of gender-stereotyped roles – who is shown doing what, or which pronouns or nouns are used. It lies at the heart of
home economics; it relates to concepts of domestic labour as a service
which a subordinate group provides.

As most references to boys' participation make clear, whatever boys have learned to do they almost always learned for themselves. They knew they were not learning how to service others, except sometimes in the context of paid employment. The 'servicing' aspect of home economics, recently re-emphasised by the GCSE National Criteria, was absent from courses geared for boys, but it runs throughout the new home economics syllabuses and textbooks, just as it did in the earliest versions. There never was much mention of fun.

As home economics is already as thoroughly male-defined as anything else in the curriculum, there can be no route to radical social transformation through making it more friendly to boys. The problem of home economics is still primarily a girls' problem: how they can secure access to an education which is *not* geared towards their subordination. It is a problem of who has the power, not who has the craft skills. Unless we seriously believe that men have left the burden of most domestic chores to women simply because they do not know how to do them, there is little point in concentrating educational resources on boys instead of girls when girls already receive less than their fair share.

It has always been open to men to step into the supposedly female-dominated domains of home economics: they have simply shown less interest in fields which are unpaid or exceptionally low-paid, and lacking in status. There has been little to stop them becoming paediatricians, gynaecologists, chefs, clothing designers or even lecturers and researchers in home economics if they wished. Yet paediatricians have sometimes made bad fathers, and men who know how to cook for themselves have declined to do so. It is too wildly hopeful to assume that explaining to men the necessity for sharing and caring, which they have not realised until now, will cause them to abandon their abuses of power. In the last resort equality is not real if it can be chosen by some and not others. Educating boys to equal roles they can still refuse is a less urgent task than empowering girls, who still have far less choice.

7

Mission and Fantasy: Influencing Girls

In 1989, while I was working on this book, a Michelle Shocked record called 'When I Grow Up' was on the radio, a funny and uncomfortable song mocking the romantic dream of marriage and motherhood. 'We're gonna have one hundred and twenty babies', ran the words of one line.*

Young women don't all dream of marriage and motherhood. If they do, their dreams conflict and shift. They may find it hard to say what they want, but know what they don't want. It may be easy to imagine girls who take optional child development courses as keen for motherhood, interested in babies if not sentimental about them, and willing to see it as a subject closely related to their personal futures. A surreal conversation I had with a group of girls in one lesson reminded me that nothing about preparing for oppressed womanhood can be so straightforward.

Sally would not at first talk about babies at all, but kept telling me about her dog. She preferred dogs to babies. Child development would help her learn how to take care of her dog: that was why she had chosen it. Her fourth-year class of twelve girls was studying a 'unit' on the care of a baby that week, writing about bathtime routines. This involved gathering information from the books and leaflets distributed around the class (including several on skin care and nappies published by the manufacturers Ashton Zorbit), cutting up a sheet of illustrations to paste into their own work, and filling in a worksheet: 'Have the bath on a firm ... with the trolley conveniently placed at your right hand'; 'Com-

---

* 'When I Grow Up', PolyGram Songs Inc., 1988.

plete the list of items to have ready on a tray.'

I asked one group of pupils if they could tell me something about the course. The conversation then ran as follows:

LISA: Child development.

LEE: It's about bathtime. You've got to cut them out.

SALLY: I wouldn't like to wash a baby, I think I'd drop it.

LEE: I like this course 'cos it's really straightforward and you find out about things yourself so that I think it's the best course you can do. We learn at the same time we're doing the course, it's really good. I think it's a brilliant course myself it's really good, it's really interesting. I like the class very much.

Later, after an interval of discussion more related to the work in hand, the teacher came over and – for my benefit – initiated another conversation about the course, what they thought of it and why they had chosen it:

LEE: I like children, but I wouldn't have them for a long, long time.

SALLY: I don't want one.

TEACHER: Good job your mum wanted one or you wouldn't be here.

SALLY: I'd drown it, I'd just put it in ... I don't want to be here, I'd rather die.

TEACHER: You don't mean that.

SALLY: What are kids for?

[Teacher moves away. General discussion amongst pupils about location of family planning clinics]

LEE [to Lisa or Sally]: Your mum having a baby?

SALLY: I'd kill it if she had one. I'd put it under the sunbed to give it a nice tan. If my baby comes out too light I'd put it under the sunbed.

Sally's teacher thought she had been showing off, and said so. It was obviously true that Sally had been acting up for the benefit of my tape-recorder, but then so had Lee, who made what was virtually a speech in praise of child development straight into the microphone. I cannot attempt to disallow the effect of my presence in this lesson, or the pupils' exhibitionism; nor can I interpret the detail of Sally's references to the sunbed, her mother or her dog except in the broadest sense. Yet although some of the content of this extract is beyond the scope of my analysis, it prompts questions and suggests themes which are echoed elsewhere.

I did not stir responses like this in any other class, so it was probably not my presence and questions alone which so unsettled the pupils. I met these same pupils in a practical 'Home Economics: Food' lesson and their behaviour was entirely different. In home economics lessons in other schools, including child development practical lessons where pupils were making wooden toys, no one reacted to my questions so noticeably. In the context of a lesson about caring for baby, it seems likely that the standard questions I asked all the pupils I spoke to in home economics lessons – what the course was about and why they had chosen it – became much more personal and disturbing. The teacher's intervention goaded Sally into her most vehement expressions, but on this occasion the questions which I had intended as neutral could have been heard as a provocation too.

Sally's theme was resistance. She would not admit to any interest in babies at all, and considering that she had presumably chosen to study child development the violence of her refusal was extraordinary. She either substituted 'dog' for baby or in each consecutive reference to a baby claimed that she would drop it, not want it, drown it, kill it and put it under a sunbed. When I asked what pupils would be doing later in the course, Sally's answer was: 'We'll be making a toy and I'll be giving it to my dog 'cos she likes teddies ...' She was certainly aiming to shock, but her statements were not random; they were organised around a consistent theme of refusal and resistance. That this was deliberate deviancy was confirmed by the reaction of her teacher, who remonstrated with Sally's mildest remark:

SALLY: I don't want one.
TEACHER: Good job your mum wanted one ...

Wanting a baby of your own, then, is implicit in studying child development. It is normal to say so, and deviant to disagree. But it is difficult for girls to say that this is what they want, even if they do think it is. Lee, who made a point of talking to me seriously and earnestly about child development, explaining her career ambitions at length, put the wanting forward into a distant future. Many girls, not only in this class, spoke of their ambitions to become nannies or work with children, but hardly any spoke of becoming mothers themselves.

Girls in home economics lessons appear to move in and out of adult roles, just as in the lesson described above they spoke alternatively of being the young daughters of their mothers, and of their own potential motherhood. This movement between adult femininity and childhood or adolescence recalls the conflict Barbara Hudson (1984) described teenage girls as experiencing, caught between the discourses of femininity and of adolescence. Adolescence, according to Hudson, is a masculine construct, at odds with femininity as constructed in present society. Girls cannot behave like 'typical' adolescents – moodily, recklessly, selfishly, rebelliously – without infringing the dictates of femininity. Yet if their behaviour conformed to models of correct femininity, they would not escape criticism – when girls act like adult women they can still seem deviant, delinquent, old-fashioned or stupidly passive. 'Whatever we do, it's always wrong', in the words of one fifteen-year-old quoted by Hudson (p. 31).

In classrooms and in home economics texts, girls are sometimes addressed as if they were already making adult decisions; at other times material is carefully designed to appeal to the interests adolescent girls are supposed to have. A pupil in one class I observed was deciding on the focus for an assignment about cookers when her teacher engaged her in a conversation about the comparative merits of microwave and conventional ovens. The teacher was urging her to see it as a *real* question: 'Which would you choose, if you could only have one? I'm not sure which one I'd choose ...'

In mock woman-to-woman situations like these, girls are very clearly placed as rehearsing for adult roles, reminded that a decision which might already be real for the teacher will be theirs to take soon. If girls go along with this, their images of themselves may be threatened and they may invite the contempt of some of their peers and even of some teachers. If they don't, their resistance is likely to bring them into collision with the aims of the courses they are taking.

Resistance, in the classes I saw, most often took the form of attempts to subvert the course content. One fourth-year girl, for example, was designing a survey of smokers' and non-smokers' diets to show that the diets of girls who smoked were more likely to meet the dietary goals promoted in home economics lessons. She was able to do this, and her teacher seemed to feel powerless to stop her, because of the current emphasis in textbooks, syllabuses and much teaching on reducing fat, sugar and salt in the diet – advice usually framed with adult men and the women feeding them in mind, rather than adolescent girls who are already watching their weight.

In other more constructive attempts at subversion, girls challenged their teachers quite openly. One pupil in a class I observed had decided to base an assignment on the experiences and care of Black children with sickle cell anaemia, although her teacher refused to give her any encouragement; another had decided to interview survivors of sexual abuse. Both these girls spoke positively about home economics, in spite of their clashes with the teacher: they knew what they wanted to do, thought the course gave them an opportunity and were not prepared to let any syllabus constraints stop them.

Stories I heard from older girls and women who had studied earlier versions of home economics told of direct and destructive resistance. In their recollections, dolls came in for a hard time and food was messed about with or spoiled, not in fun but in anger – pastry thrown at the ceiling, food deliberately burnt or thrown away, dishes chosen for practical exams which the examiner could be guaranteed not to like. These accounts seem to me to be related, not only to Sally's deviancy but to a phenomenon I noticed many times when I spoke to other women about this book. As soon as I explained that it was on home economics they would look wary, their faces closed, expressing only a polite interest. On hearing the title their expressions changed completely, and we could begin to talk.

Girls' responses may include joyless conformity, defiance or shut-in anger, but still something draws many to choose home economics courses. The evidence points to a lack of real choice for some girls, but for others there was an attraction, an appeal to which they responded. Home economics offers girls fantasy: not the trite romantic dream of husband and baby, but a more easily grasped materialist, consumerist fantasy. Girls don't have to dwell on marriage and motherhood itself so much as on a dream of the related shopping trips: adornment and acquisition, the ancient distractions. This is a dream which has not been purged from home economics. It is encouraged rather than forbidden, and allows girls to express desire without sacrificing their sense that they are still young and still themselves.

In the newer courses the emphasis on projects and surveys, combined with the amount of attention now paid to consumer studies, reinforces materialism as the basis of home economics. The human needs listed in the GCSE National Criteria are physical, economic, social and aesthetic: people as consumers. Emotional needs are not part of the list – desire cannot be mentioned. 'Needs replace desire', wrote Valerie Walkerdine in her critique of primary-school pedagogies (1986, p. 59), which have many parallels with the situation home economics teachers have always been placed in. One of their tasks now is to make sensible consumers out of adolescent girls; but desire does not simply disappear, rationalised away in favour of *Which?* magazine and the practice of drawing up comparative charts.

The store-catalogue comparative-survey approach to life which home economics currently promotes meets its response in the materialist fantasies of adolescents, girls particularly. They do not in reality have large sums of money to spend, yet they are encouraged to pretend or fantasise that they do in the cause of learning to make decisions and rational, sensible choices. Girls leaf through magazines and advertisements to 'choose' what they would buy and then list, with reasons, what they would pick for their bedrooms or their dream kitchens, even down to the colour trim on the dishwasher they want. The best part of child development, according to one girl, was learning what you need to buy for a baby. Some course books advocate sending off for catalogues from stores such as Habitat and Laura Ashley to provide pupils with source material for their work, and it is quite usual for teachers to include Mothercare catalogues and advertising leaflets amongst their teaching materials.

In early domestic economy textbooks, husbands are not mentioned except as distant reasons for a woman's existence; children rarely appear. Analysing textbooks now, there is a difference: children and spouses are there, but juxtaposed with flats, houses, menus, domestic appliances, as if all are waiting together to be chosen and acquired. Heterosexuality is the absolute norm, though – no choice allowed there.

Sometimes there is an effort to relate consumerism to adolescent interests, rather than to future adulthood – discussing the merits of different textiles when choosing an outfit to wear at the disco, or planning the food and decorations for a party (SEG, 1987, p.28). This attempt at introducing adolescents to sensible adult habits appears to deny the basis for adolescent fantasy – desire, not need – but this unacknowledged fantasy is used to draw girls in. It provides them, like the sweets used in a 'value for money' lesson described in an earlier chapter, with an immediate experience they can enjoy.

Links with commerce and industry have recently caused teachers some embarrassment, since the extent of commercial influence on home

economics in schools is well beyond anything experienced in other subject areas. NATHE has explicitly encouraged commercial involvement
(Higgins, 1985) and one large company selling dairy products and fats
sponsors an award scheme for pupils.

In the last few years, campaigners monitoring the food industry's attempts to minimise the damage done to its interests by nutrition education have begun to question the neutrality and harmlessness of the
quantities of literature it produces for classroom use. Teachers have had
a ready defence: they have relied on free posters and booklets to brighten
up their classrooms and offer pupils a range of resources because their
departments were under-resourced. In a recent radio interview a
NATHE spokeswoman insisted that biased information would be weed-
ed out, or that pupils would be encouraged to spend lesson time verify-
ing or challenging the truth of what they read. This account of the use
of commercially produced materials seems at best naive. Without exception, pupils in the classes I observed used commercial literature un-
critically and in some cases had to rely on it as their main source of
information.

The shiny imagery of new machines and just-painted bedsits is relatively recent. It is at odds with an older image of home economics as a subject with a mission, dealing with the poor and the squalid and looking
to improve the quality of life for future generations. Arguments about
the need for home economics to feature in the national curriculum, with
their warnings about pupils becoming abusive parents or failing to feed
themselves properly, echoed earlier claims about the place of domestic
subjects teaching being to 'rescue' the poor.

Past teachers and authors saw themselves as virtual missionaries.
Elizabeth Rice warned girls that women's ignorance of the theory and
practice of cookery was responsible for male drunkenness:

> A proper supply of well-cooked food, as far as the means will admit, will not
> be the least of the many attractions to husbands and sons to be found in our
> model home. In some homes, on a cold day, a dinner of bread and butter
> with a little tea will be provided, and the husband will go shivering back to
> his work, unsatisfied and unwarmed. It is not a matter of surprise that the
> attractions of the public house should sometimes prove too great for these
> hard-worked, ill-fed men. (1885, p. 122)

The mission has been international, starting with unashamed colonial ventures and continuing with schemes financed by organisations such as UNESCO, VSO, the FAO (the UN Food and Agriculture Organisation). The export of home economics, claimed to save lives, has had questionable consequences. Along with their skills and knowledge, home economists took a domestic ideology and a model of women's dependence, which they are now – in some if not all cases – beginning to reassess. Barbara Rogers (1980), in an account of the 'domestication of women' in developing countries, described how educational or training projects for women financed from abroad commonly included compulsory 'home-science' elements, regardless of whether such courses were relevant to the work women actually did. The effect was often to deprive them of equal educational and employment opportunities and force them into dependency on men.

The great problem with the concept of home economics as rescue work is that evidence to support its usefulness to the poor and needy hardly exists. Emma Goldman once wrote that the poor did not need to be told how to eat; if they only had the means to feed themselves, they could manage well enough without advice. Others looking at the relationship between the dietary advice offered to the poor and their ability to respond to it have drawn similar conclusions. Maud Pember Reeves gave her report of the findings of the Fabian women's group investigating the lives of working-class Lambeth women in 1913 the title 'Round about a pound a week', a reference to the amount of money the women surveyed had to live on. Middle-class writers had offered plenty of advice to working-class women on budgeting, thrifty cookery and keeping within their means. Reeves's findings showed that such advice was irrelevant and based on a fundamental lack of understanding of the realities of life for many women, who were often unable to choose what to buy or cook since their husbands' preferences had to be seen to first.

Bayliss and Daniels (1988) also related the apparent failure of cookery teaching to have an impact on the nutritional status of poorer women, to their status within the family – 'the family would be fed first and the mother last; training in food preparation and nutrition had a very limited effect on this situation' (p. 36). They described the drive to make domestic economy and cookery teaching more effective in the wake of the Physical Deterioration Report of 1904 as over-optimistic, taking too little account of poverty as the 'prime controller' of nutrition standards.

It is a point which needs to be made repeatedly – that the poor are generally making the most of their means already, have had to learn how, and should not be blamed for suffering the effects of poverty which they have not invited on themselves. A 1986 report on the impact of poverty on food (Cole-Hamilton and Lang) explained yet again that consumers who have least to spend must contrive to get the best value for money and usually have to buy calories in their cheapest form, which means they are literally unable to provide themselves with a healthy diet and still get enough to eat.

Home economics wants to make pupils apply what they have learned, rather than just learn about nutrition as an academic exercise. The boy who made a lentil pie was supposed to eat it, and learn to like it. There is an implied message that it is the poor who need to be changed, rather than the world they live in.

Home economics teachers, in conversation with me about their pupils, tended to speak as if girls generally came from poor homes, emotionally if not literally impoverished. A girl's level of skill was seen as reflecting badly on her mother, regardless of whether it was minimal or advanced. Teachers spoke pityingly of girls who cooked for and cared for their siblings, as if this was evidence of maternal incompetence. They spoke just as pityingly of girls whose mothers apparently did not let them into the kitchen and were equally neglectful in some other way.

Girls really could not win: they were either precociously skilled because they came from feckless homes, or deplorably unskilled because they had been deprived of maternal attention. Whatever their backgrounds, home economics offered rescue and normality and in effect aimed to put their mothers right – the explicit purpose of the domestic economy pioneers, now reappearing in assignments which require pupils to analyse the meals they eat at home to see whether they are good enough.

Even if it rarely achieved its intended effects – a teacher writing to *Housecraft* in the 1970s wondered if anyone had ever been back to check whether 3B were making a hash out of feeding their families on the wages their husbands brought home, or whether any of their training had stuck – home economics, through its very existence, has affected women's lives.

The feminist debate about domestic labour has centred on issues such as the role of housework in the economy, on how it should be recognised and rewarded or fairly shared out. It is usually taken for granted that we all know what housework means, but in fact definitions vary widely. It has been taken to mean (particularly by the maverick group Wages for Housework) all the servicing women provide for men; by materialist feminists such as Christine Delphy, it is taken to mean strictly necessary, productive though unpaid-for labour; for Marxist feminists it means the reproduction of the labour force. Yet women know that work claimed to be essential can in fact be useless, servicing nobody but simply filling up time which would otherwise be empty.

Housework is not only the essential work done mostly by women without pay; it is also a collection of imposed routines, a way of life for some women and a source of horror for others who were luckier. My own horror story is of seeing, as I drove into a small town, a middle-aged woman sweeping the road beyond the pavement in front of her house.

These useless routines, rules and norms had an origin somewhere. Home economics teaching is only one vehicle amongst many for creating and communicating an ideology of domestic labour, but it has the peculiar power which comes from being established as an expert source. Decades of teaching have had an effect on how women have come to perceive themselves and their abilities, in relation to the models of domestic labour constructed within home economics. In the early years it was not seen as problematic for teachers to instruct pupils in 'skills' and 'correct' methods and routines. That has changed, but the normative structure has not. The rules are still there in disguise.

In her study of the sociology of housework, Ann Oakley (1974) discussed the concepts of standards and routines and how these affect the lives and self-esteem of the women she interviewed. Oakley described how women define housework rules for themselves, and commented:

> Psychological reward is derived from simple adherence to standards and routines which, although originally emanating from the housewife as worker, take on an *objective* quality. Of course women do not define these housework rules in isolation from other influences. Media advertising almost certainly has an effect, and so does the prior socialization of women for domesticity ... (p.105)

Oakley made no mention of home economics teaching, but it has had precisely the effect of establishing an idea of *objective* rules about housework. Any woman born in Britain or educated here in the last hundred years or so knew – or knows – that housework is an object of study in school, with all that implies about standards and correctness. Women do not need to have studied home economics at any time in their lives to know that 'objective' standards of housework are supposed to exist, and be affected by that knowledge.

No new basis for the subject – whether it emphasises needs, issues, a rational provision of appropriate services or the learning of practical skills for living – can hope to escape playing its part in the continual re-creation of an ideology of housework. Parents or other significant adults in a child's life also inculcate similar values, but with the important difference that these are identified with specific individuals or groups rather than presented as objective. But home economics cannot incorporate subjectivity, only nod in its direction. However open-ended they try to be, textbooks and examination papers continue to refer to an implied framework of rules, a codified system of domestic knowledge and practice.

The use of numbered points reinforces this: pupils are frequently asked to give a set number of answers. They might be required to list six rules to be followed when planning meals for the family; suggest three ways of making family mealtimes happy occasions; list eight interesting sandwich fillings; name six safety precautions to take before having a party for six-year-olds; give four points which must be considered when purchasing material for curtains for a family living-room; say what four points should be considered when spending money on special bargain offers of food (all examples from papers set in the 1980s).

A few years ago a couple interviewed on a radio programme about modern marriages based on equal partnerships were asked who did which domestic chores. The husband never hung out the washing, and explained that this was because he had never been taught how to do it, unlike his wife. She attacked his explanation as a ridiculous excuse, since she had never been taught how to do it either. Perhaps, he suggested, she had somehow picked up the knowledge, as girls do when they potter about with their mothers: she denied that too. On the face of it, his belief – if genuine – that he lacked the right training to be able to hang out washing was absurd, but in fact hanging out the washing is an activity which has been taught formally to girls in the past, complete with its own set of rules.

The recent examination question requiring pupils to list four important points to consider when sorting the family wash continues the theme of regulation evident in Rice's instruction to girls, nearly a hundred years earlier: 'Give two directions to be attended to in hanging out clothes to dry' (1885, p. 62). The point is not that women really are following sets of rules as they hang out their washing to dry, but that they often suspect that the rules exist and that what they are doing is wrong. The anger and dislike many women who were formerly taught it feel towards home economics arises partly out of a sense that it has tried to regulate their lives: criticising them if they are mothers, discounting them if they are not, and suggesting that a set of happy faces round the tea table could be theirs if only they applied the right know-how. The best antidote to the guilt of betrayal which held me back as I started to write this book has been the encouragement of former pupils, women who wanted it to voice their own protest against the undermining of their own knowledge and skills in favour of a sterile system of rules without any worthwhile application.

Taking on equal opportunities, home economics has even produced a new set of rules about sharing the chores out fairly: pupils are asked to say, for instance, how they would organise a household's domestic tasks so that everyone had a reasonable amount of free time. This is of course no real redistribution of roles; it is entirely contradictory to require women, or pupils in their imaginary future roles, to ensure that responsibilities are shared. Running a well-organised equal-opportunities household becomes yet another expectation laid on good pupils and new model housewives.

To the anger, protest and resentment, home economics has made two replies. It asks that the sins of its mothers should not be visited on it, now that it has utterly changed; it accepts that some people can manage their domestic lives without formal instruction, but asks that pupils who would otherwise enjoy and achieve little in school should still be allowed to learn from it, since what it offers is particularly valuable for them.

As long as it exists as a separate subject area, home economics can never claim to have left its past behind. Built on the concepts of subordination and of the separate sphere of 'home' as the site of family life and female labour, its damaging effects on education as a whole outweigh any positive achievements. Every argument used to promote its continuation has been an indictment of the current system of schooling – the need for girls to have separate protected spaces; the need for boys to be civilised or for science and technology to be humanised; for the most vulnerable groups of pupils to gain something from compulsory education rather than leave it having gained nothing at all.

The fragmentation home economics teachers have for so long feared and fought against would be the best outcome: for the elements in its content of undeniable value (such as nutrition education, welfare legislation, the facts of childbirth) to be taught to all pupils rather than select groups – as connected to, rather than separate from, the whole of education; for mainstream science to be humanised; for all pupils to enjoy learning and practising craft skills.

I have argued that home economics has been taught to girls intensively and systematically in Britain for a long while without producing any established improvement in the quality of their later lives. It has kept girls' education inferior and their expectations low, depressing girls' and women's self-esteem. Meanwhile many other people who were never taught it, being richer, more privileged, and often male, have managed their lives well enough. *Have they? where's your proof?*

For all its rhetoric, home economics has failed to empower the weak and vulnerable and failed to advance women towards greater control of their lives. *But is that its aim?* For that, girls most urgently need an education which will give them the means to support themselves without dependency; enable them to respect themselves, their skills, knowledge and understanding of the world as in no way inferior to those of the boys who grew up with them. It has changed, but home economics is still recognisably itself – this book is not yet *in memoriam*. With so much else changing in education, now would be a good time to take it apart for good, see it as a piece of history which should no longer be allowed to shackle girls' and boys' education.

Bibliography

Adams, C. and Arnot, M. (1986) *Investigating Gender In Secondary Schools*. ILEA

Antonouris, George (1987) 'Identifying racism', *Modus*, vol. 5, no. 7, October

Arnot, Madeleine (1984) 'How shall we educate our sons?', in Deem, Rosemary (ed.) *Co-education Reconsidered*. Open University Press

Askew, Sue and Ross, Carol (1988) *Boys don't cry: Boys and Sexism in Education*. Open University Press

Associated Examining Board (AEB) (1986) *GCE Examiners' Report 1986*

Association of Teachers of Domestic Subjects (ATDS) (1911) *Suggestions on the 'Teaching of Housecraft' in Secondary Schools Offered by the Special Committee Appointed to Consider this Subject*, May

ATDS (1961) 'Memorandum of Evidence to the Committee on Higher Education' [unpublished document]

ATDS (1967) *A Survey of the Teaching of Domestic Science in Secondary Schools in England and Wales*

ATDS Curriculum Development Committee (1971) 'Lifeline?' *Housecraft*, June

ATDS (1980) 'A positive challenge', *Times Educational Supplement*, 31 October

Attar, Dena (1986) 'A dabble in the mystery of cookery', *Petits Propos Culinaires*, no. 24, November

Attar, Dena (1987) *A Bibliography of Household Books Published in Britain 1800–1914*. Prospect Books

Baldwin, Dorothy (1983, reprinted twice 1984) *All About Children: An Introduction to Child Development*. Oxford University Press

Barker, Celia, Kimmings, Sue, and Phillips, Charmian (1989) *Focus on Home Economics: A Modular Approach*. Causeway Press

Baylis, Thomas (1857) *The rights, duties and relations of domestic servants*. Sampson Low, Son & Co.

Bayliss, Robert and Daniels, Christine (1988) 'The Physical Deterioration Report of 1904 and Education in Home Economics', *History of Education Society Bulletin*, vol. 41, Spring

Bell, Jessica (1987) 'In a class of its own', *Modus* vol. 5, no. 7

Bidder, Marion Greenwood and Baddeley, Florence (1901, reprinted 1911) *Domestic Economy in Theory and Practice*. Cambridge University Press

Boult, Janet and Gull, Barbara (1989) 'The new Oxford A/AS level', *Modus*, vol. 7, no. 3, April

Brockman, A. T. (1971) 'In a boys' school curriculum', *Housecraft*, June

Broome, Angela (1989) 'The President's New Year Message', *Modus*, vol. 7, no. 1, January

Brunner, Eric (1985) *Catering for whom? A survey report on catering education in the London area 1985*. London Food Commission

Bryant, Margaret (1979) *The Unexpected Revolution*. University of London Institute of Education

Burnett, John (1974) *Useful Toil: Autobiographies of Working People from the 1820s to the 1920s*. Allen Lane

Campbell, Gillian (1985) 'Time for a change of name?' *Times Educational Supplement*, 19 April

Campbell, Janet (1910) 'Memorandum on the teaching of infant care and management in public elementary schools', Circular 758: Medical Department, Board of Education

Cartwright, Thomas (1900) *Domestic science: the science of domestic economy and hygiene treated experimentally*. Thomas Nelson and Sons

Christian-Carter, Judith (1985) 'A brave new world?' *Times Educational Supplement*, 19 April

Christian-Carter, Judith (1986) *Home Economics in Action: Food*. Oxford University Press

Clark, Margaret (1970) *Teaching cookery*. Pergamon

Cole-Hamilton, Isobel and Lang, Tim (1986) *Tightening Belts: A Report on the Impact of Poverty on Food*. London Food Commission

Coles, Jan (1987) 'Good Practice', *Modus*, vol. 5, no. 4, May

Collymore, Yvonne (1974) 'Teaching home economics in multi-cultural schools', *Housecraft*, February–June

Crease, Bethea (1965) *Careers in Catering and Domestic Science*. The Bodley Head

Daniels, Christine (1980) 'Tracing the changes', *Times Educational Supplement*, 31 October

David, Miriam E. (1980) *The State, the Family and Education*. Routledge & Kegan Paul

Davin, Anna (1979) ' "Mind that you do as you are told": reading books for board school girls, 1870–1902', *Feminist Review*, no. 3

Delamont, Sara (1978) 'The contradictions of ladies' education', in Delamont, Sara and Duffin, Laura, *The Nineteenth-Century Woman: Her Cultural and Physical World*. Croom Helm

Dent, H.C. (1977) *The Training of Teachers in England and Wales 1800–1975*. Hodder & Stoughton

DES (1987) *Education Statistics in the United Kingdom*

Department of Education and Science (DES) (1988) *Statistical Bulletin: English School Leavers 1986–87*, December

DES and Welsh Office (1989) *Design and Technology for Ages 5 to 16: Proposals of the Secretary of State for Education and Science and the Secretary of State for Wales*

DHSS (1984) *Diet and Cardiovascular Disease. Report of the Committee on the Medical Aspects of Food Policy* (COMA). HMSO

Dick, Philip (1971) 'What do the boys think about it?', *Housecraft*, June

Digby, Anne and Searby, Peter (1981) *Children, School and Society in Nineteenth-Century England*. Macmillan

Dimock, Jane (1989) 'Home economics for all', *Modus*, vol. 7, no. 3, April

Dodd, T. (1978) *Design and Technology in the School Curriculum*. Hodder & Stoughton

Domestic Economy for the Use of Schools (1878) David Bryce and Son

Dyhouse, Carol (1981) *Girls Growing up in Late Victorian and Edwardian England*. Routledge & Kegan Paul

Edwards, Derek and Mercer, Neil (1987) *Common Knowledge: The Development of Understanding in the Classroom*. Methuen

Ehrenreich, Barbara and English, Deirdre (1979) *For Her Own Good: 150 Years of the Experts' Advice to Women*. Pluto Press

Ellwood, G. (1971) 'Middle school common course', *Housecraft*, June

EOC (1987) *Facts that figure in equal opportunities and education*. Equal Opportunities Commission

Evans, John and Davies, Brian (1988) 'The rise and fall of vocational education', in Pollard, Andrew, Purvis, June and Walford, Geoffrey (eds) *Education, Training and the New Vocationalism*. Open University Press

Faunthorpe, Reverend J. P. (1881) *Household Science: Readings in necessary knowledge for girls and young women*. Edward Stanford

Finch, Irene (1987) 'Searching questions: investigatory work and GCSE', *Times Educational Supplement*, 20 February

Forbes, Peter and Gillett, Cynthia (1971) 'Food for the boys', *Housecraft*, November

Fothergill, John Milner (1881) *Domestic economy for schools*. Wm. Isbister

Fritz, Ann (1989) 'The changing face of textile studies in New South Wales', *Modus*, vol. 7, no. 3, April

Fuller, John (1962; 2nd edn 1966) *Chef's Manual of Kitchen Management*. Batsford

Geen, A.G. (1989) 'Equal Opportunities in the Curriculum: the case of home economics,' *Gender and Education*, vol. 1, no. 2

Gentlewoman, The (1864) Chapman & Hall

Gillett, Cynthia (1971) 'Teaching young men in FE', *Housecraft*, June

Gillett, Cynthia (1974) 'Multiracial education: need and innovation', *Housecraft*, May

Grafton, T. *et al.* (1983) 'Gender and curriculum choice: a case study', in Hammersley, Martyn and Hargreaves, Andy, *Curriculum Practice: Some Sociological Case Studies*. Falmer

Grant, Martin (1983) 'Craft, Design and Technology', in Whyld, Janie (ed.) *Sexism in the Secondary Curriculum*

Greenhalgh, Jan (1989) 'Home Economics and the National Curriculum', *Modus*, vol. 7, no. 4, May

Hargreaves, Winifred (1966) *Education for Family Living*. Blackwell

Harrison, William Jerome (1882) *The science of home life: a text-book of domestic economy*. T. Nelson and Sons

Hesmondhalgh, Zoe and Timpson, Maggie (1987) 'The unholy trinity is dead', *Modus*, September

Higgins, Peter (1985) 'Don't be a dinosaur', *Times Educational Supplement*, 19 April

Hill, Mary (1914) *Homecraft in the classroom*. Sir Isaac Pitman and Sons Ltd

Hinsley, Amy B. (1971) 'Teaching boys in a school for slow learners', *Housecraft*, June

HMI (1985) *Home Economics from 5 to 16: Curriculum Matters*, 5. HMSO

HMI Home Economics Committee (1978) *Curriculum 11–16: Home Economics*. Department of Education and Science

Hoare, Jane (1985) 'The sum of the whole', *Times Educational Supplement*, 19 April

Home Economics Committee of HM Inspectorate (1978) *Curriculum 11–16: Home Economics*

House of Commons (1981) *Second Report from the Education, Science and Arts Committee*

Housecraft, letters page, May/June 1975

Hudson, Barbara (1984) 'Femininity and adolescence', in McRobbie, Angela and Nava, Mica, (eds) *Gender and Generation*. Macmillan

Hutchinson, Vincent G. (1979) 'Focus on home and family', in UNESCO *New Trends in Home Economics Education*, vol. 1

Ingham, Mary (1981) *Now We Are Thirty*. Methuen

Jaques, James (1971) 'What do the boys think about it?', *Housecraft*, June

Jepson, Margaret (1987) 'Critical skills', TES, 20 February

Joint Matriculation Board Examinations Council (1986) *GCE Examiners' Reports 1986: Home Economics*

Jones, Brenda (1987) 'A change of image: from needlework to textile design', *Times Educational Supplement*, 20 February

Kelly, Alison (1985) 'The construction of masculine science', *British Journal of Sociology of Education*, vol. 6, no. 2

Kelly, Alison *et al.* (1987) 'Traditionalists and trendies; teachers' attitudes to educational issues', in Arnot, Madeleine and Weiner, Gaby (eds) *Gender Under Scrutiny: New Inquiries in Education*. Hutchinson

Lewis, Jane (1986) *Labour and Love: Women's Experience of Home and Family 1850–1940*. Basil Blackwell

Ling, Eva M. (1981, first published 1972) *Modern Household Science*. Bell & Hyman

London and East Anglian Group for GCSE Examinations, *GCSE Syllabus for schools and colleges only. Summer 1988 Home economics: Child Development, Food, Home & Family, Textiles*

Longman's Domestic Economy Readers (1910, first published 1896) Longmans, Green & Co.

McBride, Theresa M. (1976) *The Domestic Revolution: The Modernisation of Household Service in England and France 1820–1920*. Croom Helm

McGrath, Helen (1980) *About the House: An Introduction to Home Economics*. Oxford University Press

McGrath, Helen (1986, first published 1982) *All About Food: Practical Home Economics*. Oxford University Press

McIntosh, Enid (1955) 'The teaching of housecraft in the schools of today' in Weddell, Margaret (ed.) *Training in Home Management*

Mahony, Pat (1985) *Schools for the Boys? Coeducation Reassessed*. Hutchinson

Major, Henry (1893) *Little mothers: a reading-book for girls in domestic economy*. Blackie and Son Ltd

Major, Henry (1893) *The teacher's manual of lessons on domestic economy*. Blackie and Son Ltd

Major, Henry (1899) *Newmann's domestic economy for teachers*. O. Newmann & Co.

Major, Henry (1899) *Newmann's housewifery for students in cookery, laundry and house-wifery*, O. Newmann & Co.

Manthorpe, Catherine (1985) 'Socio-historical perspectives on the scientific education of girls in nineteenth and twentieth century England', unpublished PhD thesis, University of Leeds

Manthorpe, Catherine (1986) 'Science or domestic science?', *History of Education*, vol. 15, no. 3

Marris, Isabel D. (1904) *Mistresses and maids*. Jarrold & Sons

Mennell, Stephen (1985) *All Manners of Food*. Basil Blackwell

Middlemas, Margaret and Fry, D.H. (1973) 'The identity of home economics', *Housecraft*, November

Midland Examining Group (1986) *Home Economics: Home Studies: 1988 Specimen Question Papers for the General Certificate of Secondary Education*

Millman, Val (1985) 'The new vocationalism in secondary schools: its influence on girls', in Whyte, Judith, Deem, Rosemary, Kant, Lesley and Cruickshank,

Maureen (eds) *Girl Friendly Schooling*. Methuen

Modus (1987) 'Wanted: a fuller perspective', *Modus*, vol. 5, no. 4, May

Mullard, Chris (1985) 'Multiracial Education in Britain: from assimilation to cultural pluralism', in Arnot, M. (ed.) *Race and Gender: Equal Opportunities Policies in Education*. Pergamon

Myers, Jay (1971) 'Real enthusiasm', *Housecraft*, June

National Advisory Committee on Nutrition Education (NACNE) (1983) *Proposals for Nutritional Guidelines for Health Education in Britain*. Health Education Council

NATHE (1989) *Initial Response to the Interim Report of the Design and Technology Working Group* (open letter circulated with *Modus*, vol. 7, no. 1)

Newsholme, Arthur and Scott, Margaret Eleanor (1894) *Domestic economy*. Swan Sonnenschein & Co.

Newsom, John (1948) *The Education of Girls*. Faber & Faber

Northern Examining Association (NEA) *General Certificate of Secondary Education. Home Economics: Food. Syllabus for the 1988 Examination*

Nuffield Home Economics (1985a) *People and Homes*. Hutchinson

Nuffield Home Economics (1985b) *Teachers' Guide: People and Homes*. Hutchinson

Oakley, Ann (1974) *The Sociology of Housework*. Martin Robertson

Oliver, Sue (1984) *Assessment in a Multicultural Society: Home Economics at 16+*. Longman/Schools Council

O'Sullivan, Sue (ed.) (1987) *Turning the Tables*. Sheba

Palmer, Gabrielle (1988) *The Politics of Breastfeeding*. Pandora

Pender, Margaret V. (1980) 'Catering for boys', *Times Educational Supplement*, 31 October

Pratt, Brenda (1986) 'Interacting aspects', *Times Educational Supplement*, 21 February

Pratt, J., Bloomfield, J. and Searle, C. (eds) (1984) *Option Choice: A Question of Equal Opportunity*. NFER/Nelson

Prochaska, F. K. (1980) *Women and Philanthropy in Nineteenth Century England*. Clarendon Press

Purvis, June (1985) 'Domestic subjects since 1870', in Goodson, Ivor (ed.) *Social Histories of the Secondary Curriculum*. Falmer

Ravenhill, Alice and Schiff, Catherine (eds) (1910) *Household administration: its place in the higher education of women*. Grant Richards Ltd

Reeves, Maud Pember (1979, first published 1913) *Round About a Pound a Week*. Virago

Rice, Elizabeth (1885) *Textbook of domestic economy*. Blackie and Son

Riddervold, Astri and Ropeid, Andreas (1989) 'The Norwegian Porridge Feud', *Petits Propos Culinaires*, no. 32, June

Riseborough, George (1988) 'Pupils, Recipe Knowledge, Curriculum and the

Cultural Production of Class, Ethnicity and Patriarchy: a Critique of One Teacher's Practices', in *British Journal of Sociology of Education*, vol.9, no.1

Roberts, Elizabeth (1984) *A Woman's Place: An Oral History of Working-Class Women 1890–1940*. Basil Blackwell

Rogers, Barbara (1980) *The Domestication of Women*. Kogan Page

Rose, Hilary (1986) 'Beyond masculinist realities: a feminist epistemology for the sciences', in Belier, Ruth (ed.) *Feminist Approaches to Science*. Pergamon

Scarbrough, June (1987) 'Holding the baby: coping with GCSE Child Development', *Times Educational Supplement*, 20 February

Scarbrough, June (1989) 'North America Discovered', *Modus*, vol. 7, no. 1, January

Secondary Examinations Council (SEC) (1986a) *GCSE: The National Criteria: Home Economics*

SEC (1986b) *GCSE: The National Criteria*

SEC (1986c) *Home Economics GCSE: A Guide for Teachers*

Shaw, Jennifer (1984) 'The politics of single-sex schools', in Deem, Rosemary (ed.) *Co-education Reconsidered*. Open University Press

Sillitoe, Helen (1933) *A History of the Teaching of Domestic Subjects*. Methuen

Skeggs, Beverley (1988) 'Gender Reproduction and Further Education: domestic apprenticeships', *British Journal of Sociology of Education*, vol. 9, no. 2

Smith, F. B. (1979) *The People's Health 1830–1910*. Croom Helm

Southern Examining Group (SEG) (1986) *General Certificate of Secondary Education: Home Economics: Child Development, 1988 Examination*

SEG (1987) *Home Economics: People and Homes*. Nuffield

Spain, Nancy (1948) *Mrs Beeton and Her Husband*. Collins

Spear, Margaret Goddard (1985) 'Teachers' attitudes towards girls and technology', in Whyte, Judith, Deem, Rosemary, Kant, Lesley and Cruickshank, Maureen (eds) *Girl Friendly Schooling*. Methuen

Spender, Dale (1982) *Invisible Women: The Schooling Scandal*. Writers & Readers

Stanworth, Michelle (1983) *Gender and Schooling: A Study of Sexual Divisions in the Classroom*. Hutchinson

Steedman, Carolyn (1985) 'Prisonhouses', *Feminist Review*, no. 20, Summer

Stoker, Jane (1876) *Home comfort: a complete manual of domestic economy for schools and colleges*. W. Stewart & Co.

Summerfield, Penny, (1987) 'Cultural Reproduction in the Education of Girls: a Study of Girls' Secondary Schooling in Two Lancashire Towns, 1900–50', in Hunt, Felicity (ed.) *Lessons for Life: The Schooling of Girls and Women 1850–1950*. Basil Blackwell

Tegetmeier, William (1870, 1st edn 1857) *A manual of domestic economy*. Hamilton, Adams & Co.

Tegetmeier, William (1876) *The scholar's handbook of household management and cookery*. Macmillan

Thompson, Patricia, J. (1986) 'Beyond Gender: Equity Issues for Home Economics Education', *Theory into Practice*, vol. xxv, no. 4

Tillinghast, Mary (1678) *Rare and excellent receipts*

Turnbull, Annmarie (1987) 'Learning her womanly work: The Elementary School Curriculum, 1870–1914', in Hunt, Felicity (ed.), *Lessons for Life: The Schooling of Girls and Women 1850–1950*. Basil Blackwell

University of London (1986) *GCE Ordinary Level Food and Nutrition Paper 1*, June

University of London (1986) *GCE Ordinary Level Food and Nutrition Paper 2, Practical Tests*, June

Vaines, Eleanor (1979) 'Home economics: a unified field approach', in *New Trends in Home Economics Vol. 1*. UNESCO

Wadsworth, N. (1987) 'Home economics and child development', in Myers, K. (ed.), *Genderwatch!* EOC/SCDC

Walkerdine, Valerie (1986) 'Progressive pedagogy and political struggle', *Screen*, Winter

Walkerdine, Valerie and The Girls and Mathematics Unit, Institute of Education, (1989) *Counting Girls Out*. Virago

Waring, Mary (1985) 'To Make the Mind Strong, Rather than to Make it Full': Elementary School Science Teaching in London 1870–1904', in Goodson, Ivor (ed.) *Social Histories of the Secondary Curriculum*. Falmer

Warren, Eliza (1864) *How I managed my house on two hundred pounds a year*. Houlston & Wright

Webster, Augusta (1879) *A housewife's opinions*. Macmillan

Weddell, Margaret (ed.) (1955) *Training in Home Management*. Routledge & Kegan Paul

Whitfield, Margaret (1971) 'A vocational bias', *Housecraft*, June

Whyld, Janie (ed.) (1983) *Sexism in the Secondary Curriculum*. Harper & Row

Widdowson, Frances (1980) *Going Up into the Next Class: Women and Elementary Teacher Training 1840–1914*. Hutchinson

Wigley, Mrs W. H. (1878) *Simple lessons in domestic economy, with questions for examination*. Thomas Murby

Wynn, Barbara (1983) 'Home economics', in Whyld, Janie (ed.) *Sexism in the Secondary Curriculum*

Wynn, Barbara, (1986) *Food Investigations*. Oxford University Press

Yorke, Margaret (1987) 'The President's Speech, AGM 1987', *Modus*, vol. 5, no. 6, September

Yorke, Margaret (1988) 'Breadth and balance', *Times Educational Supplement*, 18 March

Yoxall, Ailsa (1965, first published 1913) *A history of the teaching of domestic economy*. Cedric Chivers Ltd

Index

THE EDUCATION SERIES
In association with the University of London Institute of Education
Series Editor JANE MILLER

In recent years the attacks on education in Britain have meant a complete redrawing of the educational map. But attempts to stifle opposition and resistance have neither silenced nor deterred those who are doing innovatory work in every aspect of the field. In support of this radical tradition, Virago has launched a new education series, published in association with the University of London Institute of Education, committed to providing information and understanding of the social, cultural and developmental issues of significance in education today. It presents some of the most exciting and important thinking in ways which will appeal to professionals as well as to students and parents and all those for whom education is a central and continuing concern. The books are by teachers and researchers and originate from classrooms in schools and colleges, from the practices of teaching and the experiences of learning. The series' general editor is Jane Miller, Senior Lecturer in the Joint Department of English and Media Studies at the Institute of Education.

READ IT TO ME, NOW!
Learning at Home and at School

Hilary Minns

Read it to Me, Now! is a book about five four-year-olds who will all become pupils at the same primary school. It covers both the pre-school period, focussing on the children's backgrounds and their experience of reading and writing, and the first few months of school – their developing awareness of themselves as readers and writers. Hilary Minns points out that children do not arrive at school as 'non-readers', but as having unique reading histories of their own, learnt socially and culturally within their family and community. There is Gemma, from a working-class family, who, at first unused to handling books in the home, slowly changes literacy practices in the family; Gurdeep, arriving at school with a rich knowledge of sacred Sikh tales his mother heard as a girl in India; Anthony, already with a highly developed sense of narrative, learnt mainly from stories and TV dramas; Geeta, who took herself seriously as a reader long before she came to school; and Reid, arriving at school with the feeling that reading was something easily achieved. In drawing together these stories, Hilary Minns illuminatingly suggests ways towards the creation of a total literacy environment for children while recognising the individual character of each child's reading history.